SILENCING POLITICAL DISSENT

OTHER OPEN MEDIA BOOKS

9-11
Noam Chomsky
128 pages / $8.95 / ISBN: 1-58322-489-0

TERRORISM AND WAR
Howard Zinn
160 pages / $9.95 / ISBN: 1-58322-493-9

BIN LADEN, ISLAM, AND AMERICA'S NEW "WAR ON TERRORISM"
As`ad AbuKhalil
112 pages / $8.95 / ISBN: 1-58322-492-0

OPEN MEDIA PAMPHLET SERIES TITLES

ACTS OF AGGRESSION: POLICING "ROGUE" STATES
Noam Chomsky with Edward W. Said
64 pages / $6.95 / ISBN: 1-58322-546-3

ZAPATISTA ENCUENTRO
The Zapatistas
64 pages / $6.95 / ISBN: 1-58322-548-X

SECRET TRIALS AND EXECUTIONS: MILITARY TRIBUNALS
AND THE THREAT TO DEMOCRACY
Barbara Olshansky
80 pages / $6.95 / ISBN: 1-58322-537-4

10 REASONS TO ABOLISH THE IMF & WORLD BANK
Kevin Dahaner
104 pages / $6.95 / ISBN: 1-58322-464-5

SENT BY EARTH
Alice Walker
64 pages / $5.00 / ISBN: 1-58322-491-2

TERRORISM: THEIRS AND OURS
Eqbal Ahmad
64 pages / $6.95 / ISBN: 1-58322-490-4

THE UMBRELLA OF U.S. POWER
Noam Chomsky
80 pages / $6.95 / ISBN: 1-58322-547-1

**TO ORDER ADDITIONAL SERIES TITLES CALL 1 (800) 596-7437
OR VISIT WWW.SEVENSTORIES.COM**

SILENCING POLITICAL DISSENT

Nancy Chang
and the Center for Constitutional Rights

Foreword by Howard Zinn

AN OPEN MEDIA BOOK

SEVEN STORIES PRESS / NEW YORK

CONTENTS

This book is dedicated to the memory of my mother, T. C. Chang, who passed away on March 18, 2002. Her example of how an ordinary life can be conducted with extraordinary grace, purpose, and wisdom carries me forward.

In addition, this book is dedicated to my husband, Daniel Rossner, who, but for the New York primary election scheduled for September 11, 2001, would have been in his office on the fifty-eighth floor of One World Trade Center at the time that tower was struck. Dan has encouraged me both in the writing of this book and in my work for the past five and a half years as an attorney at the Center for Constitutional Rights. I am grateful to him for his love and support, and for his unwavering commitment to the Bill of Rights.

Finally, this book is dedicated to the memory of those who fell victim to the September 11 attacks and to their loved ones.

ACKNOWLEDGMENTS

I wish to thank all of my colleagues at the Center for Constitutional Rights for their tireless efforts to safeguard the Bill of Rights in the wake of September 11. This book has benefited enormously from my discussions with CCR colleagues William Goodman, Ron Daniels, Michael Ratner, Arthur Kinoy, David Cole, Abdeen Jabara, Franklin Siegel, Barbara Olshansky, Denise Reinhardt, Paul Schachter, Shayana Kadidal, Anna Liza Gavieres, and Janice Badalutz.

I also wish to thank everyone who generously volunteered their time to assist in the researching, proofreading, citation checking, and editing of this book. I am especially indebted to my dear friend of more than two decades, Barry Bennett, and to Greg Diamond, Bryan Gunderson, Julie Rivchin, Justin Weyerhaeuser, and Pavani Yalamanchili, friends I have made through the Center for Constitutional Rights's student internship program, for their outstanding and invaluable contributions.

In addition, I wish to thank the individuals with whom I have had the privilege of working toward the goal of preserving our civil liberties in the post–September 11 world. Included among their ranks are attorneys, political activists, grassroots organizers, labor organizers, lobbyists, representatives of Muslim, Arab, and South Asian communities in the United States, journalists, university professors, schoolteachers, students, firefighters, artists, and ordinary Americans. While their areas of concern are diverse, they are united in their determination to resist the rollback of our political and personal freedoms.

Finally, I wish to thank my editor, Greg Ruggiero, who founded the Open Media Pamphlet Series in 1991, and who skillfully shepherded this project through from its conception to its actualization with a boundless enthusiasm. I am grateful to Greg and to Dan Simon, the publisher of Seven Stories Press, for their support of this project, for their creative vision, and for bringing forward views not aired in the mainstream press. Their Open Media Books broaden the terms of political discourse and encourage democracy to thrive.

Nancy Chang

FOREWORD

by Howard Zinn

This analysis by Nancy Chang of the Center for Constitutional Rights should be read by everyone concerned with a free society. It reports a chilling set of rules, now the law, which directly affect millions of Americans who are not citizens, but also the rest of the population, who must live in an atmosphere of fear. Furthermore, this draconian law, worthy of a police state, is extremely unlikely to be overthrown by the courts, given the historic subservience of the courts to executive authority in time of war.

It is ironic, but a historic truth, repeated again and again, that exactly at those moments when citizens need the greatest freedom to speak their minds, exactly when life and death issues are involved, that is, when the question is war or peace, it is then that our liberties are taken away. The juggernaut of war crushes democracy, just when the nation claims it is fighting for democracy.

It becomes crucial, then, for citizens to demand their freedom to speak, to resist the power of the state when it demands unanimity and slavish obedience to the arbitrary decisions of government. In order for them to do that, they must understand the laws used to stifle their voices. They will then see that the so-called PATRIOT Act is the opposite of patriotism, if patriotism means love of your country and not the government, love of the principles of democracy and not the edicts of authority.

That is why this analysis of the new law is so important for everyone concerned with freedom.

INTRODUCTION

The September 11, 2001, attacks on the World Trade Center and the Pentagon stunned us with their stealth, their precision, their calculated cruelty, and the horrific trail of death and destruction left in their wake. They have forced us to confront our vulnerability to terrorism and to take steps to improve our nation's security. But in our desperation to feel safe, we are sacrificing the core democratic values that have guided this nation since its founding without first examining whether we are, in fact, any safer as a result.

This book examines how a number of domestic antiterrorism measures implemented in the nine months since the attacks undermine our civil liberties. By the end of October 2001, a panic-stricken Congress had acceded to the executive branch's demands for broad new powers in a major piece of legislation titled the USA PATRIOT Act. The act's broad new crime of "domestic terrorism" threatens to criminalize protest activities and stifle dissent. The enhanced surveillance powers that the act grants the executive threaten to intrude upon the privacy of everyone in the United States, even those with no ties to terrorism. And the act's authorization of mandatory detention and deportation of noncitizens based on their political activities and associations threatens to deny noncitizens their most basic constitutional rights. Before casting the lone vote in the Senate against the USA PATRIOT Act, Senator Russell Feingold of Wisconsin warned:

> Of course, there is no doubt that if we lived in a police state, it would be easier to catch terrorists. If we lived in a country that allowed the police to search your home at any time for any reason; if we lived in a country that allowed the government to open your mail, eavesdrop on your phone conversations, or intercept your email communications; if we lived in a country that allowed the government to hold people in jail indefinitely based on what they write or think, or based on mere suspicion that they are up to no good, then the government would no doubt discover and arrest more terrorists. But that probably would not be a country in which we would want to live. And that would not be a country for which we could, in good conscience, ask our young people to fight and die. In short, that would not be America. Preserving our freedom is one of the main reasons that we are now engaged in this new war on terrorism. We will lose that war without firing a shot if we sacrifice the liberties of the American people.[1]

When the Bush administration has lacked authorization from Congress for its domestic antiterrorism measures, it has authorized them by executive fiat. On the basis of interim agency rules and directives, and under cover of secrecy, the administration has interrogated without suspicion, arrested without charge, and detained without justification as many as two thousand Muslim nationals of Middle Eastern and South Asian countries. Yet to date, the only indictment for a crime directly relating to the September 11 attacks has been that of Zacarias Moussaoui, who was arrested prior to the attacks. Through these measures, the administration has all but officially sanctioned the practice of ethnic and religious profiling. The administration has also issued an interim agency rule that allows the Department of Justice to monitor privileged communications between federal detainees and their attorneys. The specter of government monitoring promises to thwart the ability of criminal defendants to receive the effective assistance of counsel to which they are entitled under the Sixth Amendment.

At the same time, the Bush administration has taken steps to silence political dissent. Attorney General John Ashcroft, the top official in charge of enforcing the laws of the United States, has challenged the patriotism of those who oppose the administration's policies. In addition, he has issued new guidelines for domestic intelligence-gathering that repeal reforms instituted in response to the Church Committee's 1976 findings that the FBI and CIA had engaged in domestic spying on lawful political activities. The administration has also engaged in a campaign to restrict access to government information that has blocked the press, the public, and even Congress in their efforts to hold the executive branch accountable for its actions.

And yet for all the harm these measures will inflict on the Bill of Rights, they are unlikely to make us safer, and could even make us less safe. A full eight months after September 11, the Bush administration was forced to back-track from its earlier denials and admit that the FBI and CIA had received several warnings that Al Qaeda network members were taking flight lessons and had plans to hijack commercial airplanes in the United States.[2] The government has admitted that its failure to heed the warnings was not because of a lack of law enforcement powers. Rather, the failure was the result of an information overload, a lack of trained translators, and communication failures within and between intelligence agencies. The recently announced reorganization of the FBI and the loosening of FBI domestic intelligence-gathering guidelines to permit monitoring of individuals not suspected of criminal activity are likely to result in an even greater overload of information. More agents will be pursuing more false leads, and more time, energy, and attention will be diverted from the warnings that we cannot afford to miss.

This book's examination of the threats to our freedom posed by these post–September 11 measures is framed at its outset by a review of the history of the Constitution in times of crisis, and at its end by a discussion of how we can halt the further erosion of the Bill of Rights. It is the author's hope that this book will inspire the reader to join the growing movement to reclaim our civil liberties.

"History teaches that grave threats to liberty often come in times of urgency, when constitutional rights seem too extravagant to endure. The World War II relocation-camp cases, and the Red Scare and McCarthy-era internal subversion cases, are only the most extreme reminders that when we allow fundamental freedoms to be sacrificed in the name of real or perceived exigency, we invariably come to regret it."

—from Justice Thurgood Marshall's dissenting opinion in *Skinner v. Railway Labor Executives' Association*, 489 U.S. 602, 635 (1989).

CHAPTER 1

THE CONSTITUTION IN TURMOIL

Born of revolution, for over two hundred years the United States Constitution has been the foundation of American stability. A nation of immigrants bound by no common language or heritage has been unified by the idea of democratic liberty, embodied in its founding document. Through civil war and world war, through Red Scare and McCarthyism, our liberties have been challenged and at times almost discarded; but ultimately the Constitution has proved a resilient guardian of our political freedoms.

The framers' genius informs the Constitution's every aspect. Its very structure embraces democratic values. The framers understood from firsthand experience that "[t]he accumulation of all power, legislative, executive, and judicial in the same hands...may justly be pronounced the very definition of tyranny."[1] By dividing the power of government among three branches—the Congress, which legislates, the president, whose responsibility it is to see that the laws are faithfully executed, and the judiciary, which ensures that the other two branches do not overstep their authority—the Constitution enforces a system of checks and balances in which each branch is positioned to check the abuse of power by the other branches.[2] As Supreme Court Justice Louis Brandeis eloquently explained, "[t]he doctrine of the separation of powers was adopted by the [Constitutional Convention] of 1787, not to promote efficiency but to preclude the exercise of arbitrary power. The purpose was not to avoid friction, but, by means of the inevitable friction incident to the distribution of the governmental powers among three departments, to save the people from autocracy."[3]

The first ten amendments to the Constitution—which collectively comprise the Bill of Rights—guarantee Americans the political freedoms and individual liberties essential to an open society. The core of the Bill of Rights is the First Amendment, which guarantees our freedoms of speech, political association, and religion, our rights to assemble peaceably and to petition the government for a redress of grievances, and the freedom of the press.[4] These guarantees encourage democratic participation in government by promoting debate on public issues that is "uninhibited, robust, and wide-open," an inquisitive press, and government accountability for its actions.[5]

The remaining amendments in the Bill of Rights safeguard us against undue governmental interference in our lives. The Fourth Amendment protects our privacy against unreasonable government intrusion and surveillance.[6] Its warrant requirement imposes a judicial check on the executive branch. Except in the case of exigent circumstances, a law enforcement officer must obtain a warrant from a neutral and independent magistrate prior to conducting a search or seizure. The warrant must be supported by the officer's written affirmation that there is probable cause to believe that a specific criminal act has taken place and that the

Nancy Chang

search or seizure that the warrant authorizes will uncover evidence of the crime.[7]

The due process clause of the Fifth Amendment demands fairness from the federal government.[8] On a substantive level, the due process clause protects us against government action "that 'shocks the conscience' or interferes with rights 'implicit in the concept of ordered liberty.'"[9] On a procedural level, the due process clause bars the government from depriving any person—whether citizen or not—of life, liberty, or property without first providing the person with a full and fair opportunity to be heard.[10] The requirement of equal protection of the laws, which the Supreme Court has read into the Fifth Amendment by way of the Fourteenth Amendment, prohibits the government from intentional discrimination on the basis of race, ethnicity, gender, religion, or political belief.[11] And the Sixth Amendment promises a fair trial and the assistance of counsel to those accused of crimes.[12]

The Bill of Rights is a permanent fixture in the American legal landscape, not a fair-weather friend. Its provisions remain in full force even during times of crisis, although the balance that is struck between competing interests is often influenced by the presence of a compelling governmental interest in the nation's security. The same holds true for the rest of the Constitution's provisions, with a single exception. Under the suspension clause, Congress is authorized to suspend the writ of habeas corpus—the procedure by which the federal courts may order the release of individuals from illegal detention—though only "when in Cases of Rebellion or Invasion the public Safety may require it."[13]

Experience has taught us, however, that holding the

Constitution to its promises is a difficult task even in the best of times; it requires exceptional vigilance, courage, and determination in times of uncertainty. As tensions mount, fear crowds out reason, while suspicion supplants fact. Under these conditions, the authoritarian impulse—the proclivity of governments to accumulate and abuse power, quash their political opponents, and cloak their operations behind a veil of secrecy—is easily unleashed from its peacetime restraints.

I. CRIMINALIZING POLITICAL DISSENT

A. THE SEDITION ACT OF 1798

Just seven years after the ratification of the Bill of Rights, the First Amendment came under assault. In an ultimately unsuccessful bid to prevent the Republican Party from gaining power, a Federalist-controlled Congress enacted the Sedition Act of 1798, which made it a crime to criticize the government.[14] Although the Federalists claimed that this extreme measure was justified in light of heightened tensions between the United States and France, curiously, all of the indictments, prosecutions, and convictions under the act were of Republicans. One of the best-known figures to be convicted under the act was a congressman, Matthew Lyon of Vermont. Lyon served a four-month prison sentence for his "crime" of describing President Adams as "swallowed up in a continual grasp for power, in an unbounded thirst for ridiculous pomp, foolish adulation, and selfish avarice."[15] The Federalists' misguided quest for political power backfired on them. Lyon and the other Republicans who had been outspoken critics of the Federalists became popular heroes and, in 1801, Thomas Jefferson, a Republican, wrested the presidency from Adams. As president, Jefferson pardoned those who had been convicted under the act.

B. THE ESPIONAGE ACT OF 1917

The worldwide political unrest of the World War I era brought forth a fresh assault on the First Amendment. The Espionage Act of 1917 made it a crime to "willfully utter, print, write, or publish any disloyal, profane, scurrilous, or abusive language" about the United States, or to "cause or attempt to cause, or incite or attempt to incite, insubordination, disloyalty, mutiny, or refusal of duty, in the military or naval forces of the United States."[16] In 1919, the Supreme Court upheld the conviction under the Espionage Act of socialist Charles Schenck, who had printed and distributed pamphlets urging opposition to the draft.[17] The Court's unanimous opinion, authored by Justice Oliver Wendell Holmes, flatly rejected Schenck's argument that his speech was protected under the First Amendment. Instead, the Court held that government may restrict speech when it presents a "clear and present danger" of "bring[ing] about the substantive evils that Congress has a right to prevent." The Court went on to declare that "[w]hen a nation is at war many things that might be said in time of peace are such a hindrance to its effort that their utterance will not be endured so long as men fight."[18]

The *Schenck* decision is perhaps best known for the Court's pronouncement that an individual who falsely shouts "fire" in a crowded theater is not protected by the First Amendment. Historian Howard Zinn has suggested that Schenck's act was more akin to someone "shouting, not falsely, but truly, to people about to buy tickets and enter a theater, that there was a fire raging inside." Zinn questions whether the war itself "was a 'clear and present danger,' indeed, more clear and present and more dangerous to life than any argument against it."[19]

The Supreme Court also upheld the conviction under the Espionage Act of socialist labor leader Eugene Debs based on an impassioned antiwar speech he delivered in Canton, Ohio, in which he counseled those in the audience of conscription age, "You need to know that you are fit for something better than slavery and cannon fodder."[20] Debs, the founder of the Industrial Workers of the World, had been sentenced to a ten-year prison term. From prison, he mounted his fifth and final presidential campaign. His sentence was commuted after thirty-two months by President Warren Harding, and he was released from prison at the age of sixty-six.[21]

C. THE SMITH ACT OF 1940

The First Amendment came under challenge once again with the passage of the Smith Act of 1940, which made it a crime to "knowingly or willfully advocate, abet, advise, or teach the duty, necessity, desirability, or propriety of overthrowing or destroying any government in the United States by force or violence," or to "organize...any...assembly of persons who teach, advocate, or encourage the overthrow or destruction of any government in the United States by force or violence."[22] In the late 1940s, as Cold War tensions between the United

States and the Soviet Union mounted, the Truman administration capitulated to the anticommunist frenzy by indicting Eugene Dennis and ten other Communist Party leaders under the Smith Act for conspiring to organize the Communist Party and for advocating the overthrow of the United States government by force and violence.[23] Following a highly contentious trial in 1949 that stretched over nine months and led to accusations of judicial bias and prosecutorial misconduct, all eleven defendants were convicted.

The Supreme Court, in a plurality opinion written by Chief Justice Frederick Vinson, upheld the convictions of Dennis and his fellow Communist Party leaders under a First Amendment test that provided even less protection of speech than the "clear and present danger" test applied in the *Schenck* case.[24] Chief Justice Vinson asked "whether the gravity of the 'evil,' discounted by its improbability, justifie[d] such invasion of free speech as is necessary to avoid the danger." Despite the fact that the Communist Party had not used force or violence, Chief Justice Vinson concluded that "[t]he formation...of such a highly organized conspiracy, with rigidly disciplined members subject to call when the [leaders] felt that the time had come for action, coupled with the inflammable nature of world conditions, similar uprisings in other countries, and the touch-and-go nature of our relations with countries with whom [the leaders] were in the very least ideologically attuned," posed a sufficiently grave danger to justify the convictions of its leaders.[25]

By the end of 1954, Senator Joseph McCarthy had been censured by the Senate, and the anticommunist hysteria that he had done so much to incite began to subside. In 1957, the Supreme Court, in *Yates v. United States*, reversed the convictions of Communist Party leaders under the Smith Act by drawing a distinction between "advocacy of abstract doctrine and advocacy directed at promoting unlawful action."[26] However, it was not until 1969, the final year of Chief Justice Earl Warren's sixteen-year tenure on the Supreme Court—a tenure remarkable for its groundbreaking decisions promoting individual freedom and racial equality—that the Court finally abandoned the cramped reading of the First Amendment adopted in the *Schenck*, *Debs*, and *Dennis* cases.

In the pivotal case of *Brandenburg v. Ohio*, the Warren Court declared that "the constitutional guarantees of free speech and free press do not permit a state to forbid or proscribe advocacy of the use of force or of law violation except where such advocacy is directed to inciting or producing imminent lawless action and is likely to incite or produce such action."[27] *Brandenburg* marked a crucial turning point in the Court's First Amendment jurisprudence by establishing that "mere abstract teaching" of "the moral propriety or even moral necessity for a resort to force and violence" cannot be prohibited. Under this new standard, the Court reversed the conviction of a Ku Klux Klan leader based on his statement at a rally for white supremacy that "if our President, our Congress, our Supreme Court, continues to suppress the white, Caucasian race, it's possible that there might have to be some revengeance [*sic*] taken."[28]

II. INTERFERING WITH THE RIGHT TO FREEDOM OF POLITICAL ASSOCIATION

A. THE COLD WAR

The ruthless witch hunt for communists and their "fellow travelers" during the height of the Cold War—from the late 1940s to the early 1950s—stands out as one of the most sordid chapters in American history. Communist Party leaders were criminally prosecuted and convicted under the Smith Act based on their political views.[29] Witnesses subpoenaed before the infamous House Un-American Activities Committee (HUAC) who refused to answer questions about their membership in the Communist Party or to supply the names of their political associates were imprisoned for contempt of Congress.[30] Federal and state government employees, attorneys seeking admission to the bar, and labor union leaders were required either to sign loyalty oaths disclaiming any association with the Communist Party or relinquish their positions.[31] "Communist-action" and "communist-front" organizations were required either to register with the attorney general, reveal the names and addresses of their officers and members, and account for financial contributions, or to face criminal penalties.[32] As anticommunist hysteria swept the nation, organizations suspected of communist ties found it increasingly difficult to retain their members, much less attract new members and raise funds. Individuals suspected of being sympathetic to leftist causes were subjected to surveillance, blacklisted from employment, and saw their reputations destroyed.

While anticommunist fervor ran high, the Supreme Court consistently deferred to the political branches of government on the question of whether restrictions on the First Amendment were justified by the threat that the Communist Party posed. Between 1945 and 1957, HUAC held "at least 230 public hearings, at which more than 3,000 persons testified, of whom 135 were cited for contempt."[33] When a court convicted former college professor Lloyd Barenblatt for contempt of Congress and sentenced him to six months in prison because he had refused to respond to HUAC questioning concerning his political beliefs and affiliations, the Supreme Court affirmed his conviction.[34] The Court found that Barenblatt's First Amendment rights were outweighed by the government's interest in "self-preservation" in a situation where Congress had found that the Communist Party was intent on overthrowing the United States government by force and violence.[35] On this reasoning, the Court affirmed the contempt convictions of civil rights activists Frank Wilkinson and Carl Braden, who, like Barenblatt, had refused to name names when subpoenaed before HUAC.[36]

For similar reasons, the Court upheld a provision of the Labor Management Relations Act of 1947 that conditioned the recognition of labor unions on their leaders' disavowal of communist ties.[37] The Court also upheld a provision of the Internal Security Act of 1950 that required the compulsory registration of communist organizations with the attorney general.[38]

In 1957, however, with its decision in *Yates*, the Supreme Court tentatively asserted itself as a check on the excesses of the political branches. In 1961, in *Scales v. United States*, the

Court overturned the Smith Act convictions of Communist Party leaders on the ground that "a blanket prohibition of association with [the Communist Party,] a group having both legal and illegal aims," would pose "a real danger that legitimate political expression or association would be impaired."[39] Similarly, in 1967, in *United States v. Robel*, the Court struck down a provision of the Internal Security Act that barred members of "communist-action" organizations from working at defense facilities. The Court objected to the provision because it "swe[pt] indiscriminately across all types of association with communist-action groups, without regard to the quality and degree of membership."[40]

The Supreme Court's decisions in *Scales* and *Robel* established what is accepted today as a basic tenet of constitutional law: guilt cannot be imposed based solely on one's association with an organization that has both lawful and unlawful ends. Instead, guilt must be personal, and it must be based on clear proof of an intent to further the unlawful ends of such an organization by resort to force or violence.[41] As Chief Justice Earl Warren observed in *Robel*, "[i]t would indeed be ironic if, in the name of national defense, we would sanction the subversion of one of those liberties—the freedom of association—which makes the defense of the Nation worthwhile."[42]

B. THE FBI'S COINTELPRO PROGRAM

Government efforts to suppress political association did not end with the ebbing of Cold War tensions. Between 1956 and 1971, the FBI operated COINTELPRO, a secret political intelligence program that covertly spied on, and interfered with, law-abiding political organizations that were engaged in activities protected by the First Amendment. The existence of COINTELPRO—shorthand for counterintelligence program—did not come to light until March 1971, when the "Citizens' Committee to Investigate the FBI" broke into an FBI field office in Media, Pennsylvania, and provided the press with documents seized from that office. The program's purposes were sinister. According to a memo written by J. Edgar Hoover—the FBI's controversial director from 1924 until his death in 1972—on May 9, 1969, COINTELPRO's mission was designed to "expose, disrupt, misdirect, discredit, or otherwise neutralize activities" of individuals and organizations perceived by the government to pose a threat to domestic interests.[43]

COINTELPRO was created in 1956 to investigate the Communist Party, but by 1961 it had turned its attention to the Socialist Workers Party.[44] With the social unrest and upheaval of the mid-1960s, COINTELPRO widened its targets to include the civil rights movement, the black nationalist movement, the white supremacist movement, the women's liberation movement, and the "New Left," which included groups opposed to the Vietnam War.[45] From 1963 until his death in 1968, Martin Luther King Jr. remained the target of a ferocious FBI smear campaign, the goal of which was to "neutralize" him as an effective civil rights leader.[46] The FBI went to the extreme of mailing Dr. King a composite audiotape of recordings picked up by microphones it had planted in hotel rooms he had occupied. The tape was accompanied by a note suggesting that Dr. King commit suicide or face the public release of the tape.[47]

In the case of the FBI's investigation of the black nationalist movement, agents were instructed to "prevent groups and leaders from gaining 'respectability' by discrediting them" and "prevent the rise of a 'messiah,'" such as Dr. King, Stokely Carmichael, or Elijah Muhammed, "who could 'unify and electrify' the movement."[48] In the case of the FBI's investigation of the New Left, agents were instructed to instigate "personal conflicts or animosities" between leaders, create the impression that leaders are "informants for the Bureau or other law enforcement agencies," "have members arrested on marijuana charges," "exploit the 'hostility' between New Left and Old Left groups," and "use 'cooperative press contacts.'"[49]

In April 1976, following a yearlong investigation, the Senate Select Committee to Study Governmental Operations with Respect to Intelligence Activities, chaired by Senator Frank Church, issued a scathing report documenting in extensive detail the FBI's abuses in its COINTELPRO operations. The Church Committee roundly condemned COINTELPRO for having accumulated, in a manner "indisputably degrading to a free society," massive intelligence information on lawful activity, including protest activity and domestic dissent, and on law-abiding citizens, for purposes "related only remotely or not at all to law enforcement and the prevention of violence."[50] The Church Committee was even harsher in its condemnation of the FBI's frequent resort to its repertoire of "dirty tricks," which included the frequent use of informants and agents provocateurs to infiltrate and disrupt political organizations, illegal wiretaps and break-ins, and the spread of false rumors that caused reputations to be ruined, jobs to be lost, and marriages and friendships to be destroyed.[51]

COINTELPRO was effective in suppressing many of the dissident political movements that burgeoned in the mid-1960s. Groups that were the targets of the FBI's clandestine actions to "expose, disrupt, misdirect, discredit, or otherwise neutralize" their activities found it difficult to maintain their cohesiveness, momentum, and ability to attract new adherents.[52] The full extent to which COINTELPRO shifted the trajectory of political life in the United States will never be known.

C. IMPOSING LIMITS ON THE FBI

Although the Church Committee proposed legislation that would have set limits on the FBI's power to surveil political activities protected by the First Amendment, Congress failed to pass it.[53] In the face of a strong public and congressional outcry over the Church Committee's finding that the COINTELPRO program was riddled with FBI misconduct, Attorney General Edward Levi in 1976 issued the first set of internal FBI guidelines establishing standards and procedures for domestic security investigations.[54] The Levi guidelines were replaced in 1983 by more permissive guidelines issued by Attorney General William French Smith.[55] As discussed in chapter 4, on May 30, 2002, the Smith guidelines were in turn replaced by even more permissive guidelines by Attorney General Ashcroft.[56]

Before the FBI was permitted to launch a "full investigation" of domestic terrorism, the Smith guidelines required the FBI to have a "reasonable indication" that "two or more persons were engaged in an enterprise for the purpose of furthering *political or social* goals wholly or in part through activities involving force or violence and a violation of the criminal laws of the United States."[57] The "reasonable indication" could consist of "an objective, factual basis" based on "specific facts or circumstances indicating a past, current, or impending violation." As the guidelines themselves readily acknowledged, this showing is "substantially lower" than the probable cause showing required under the Fourth Amendment for searches and seizures.[58]

Although the Smith guidelines stated that "[i]t is important that such investigations not be based solely on activities protected by the First Amendment or on the lawful exercise of any other rights secured by the Constitution or the laws of the United States," they added that "[w]hen...statements advocate criminal activity or an apparent intent to engage in crime, particularly crimes of violence, an investigation under these Guidelines may be warranted unless it is apparent, from the circumstances or the context in which the statements are made, that there is no prospect of harm."[59] Thus, the Smith guidelines did nothing to prohibit the FBI from conducting an investigation of an organization based solely on the statement of a single member who advocated an intent to engage in acts of civil disobedience, unless it was apparent that there was no prospect of harm — a finding that law enforcement agencies are loath to make.

The Smith guidelines permitted the FBI to infiltrate an organization under investigation through "[u]ndisclosed participation in [its activities] by an undercover [FBI] employee or cooperating private individual," even if this participation "may influence the exercise of rights protected by the First Amendment."[60] On April 19, 1995, shortly after the terrorist bombing of the Alfred P. Murrah Federal Building in Oklahoma City, FBI Director Louis Freeh testified before a House subcommittee that the FBI had relaxed the Smith guidelines, not by amending them, but by "interpreting" them to allow the commencement of a domestic terrorism investigation when the FBI has a reasonable indication that an organization advocates the future, non-imminent use of violence to achieve its political or social objectives and it is apparent that the organization has the ability to carry out its objectives.[61]

Even if the FBI lacked a reasonable indication of criminal activity, the Smith guidelines permitted it to conduct a "preliminary inquiry" to check out "an allegation or information indicating the possibility of criminal activity."[62] While falling short of a full investigation, preliminary inquiries allowed the government "to respond in a measured way to ambiguous or incomplete information."[63] Among the investigative techniques available to the FBI in a preliminary investigation were the examination of records available to the public; federal, state, and local government records; interviews of potential subjects and those who should be readily able to corroborate or deny the truth of the allegation; and physical and photographic surveillance.[64]

A separate set of attorney general guidelines governs the FBI's collection of foreign intelligence in the United States. These guidelines were issued in 1976 by Attorney General Levi and were last modified in 1995 by Attorney General Janet Reno. As is common in the case of documents that address foreign intelligence matters, the guidelines are, for the most part, classified as secret. In contrast to the Smith guidelines, the foreign intelligence guidelines permit an investigation to be opened in the absence of any suspicion of criminal conduct if the target of investigation is believed to be an agent of a foreign power.[65]

A petition signed by several hundred law professors and submitted to Congress a decade ago sounded the following warning about the chilling effect of the Smith guidelines on the exercise of First Amendment rights:

> Once an organization is under investigation based on the speech of one of its members, the [Smith G]uidelines allow the FBI to collect information about all members who participate in its demonstrations, about the structure of the organization as well as the relationship of the members, and even about other organizations that cooperate with it.... We believe that the rights of free speech and association are invariably compromised by such broad investigative power. When secret informants are introduced into political organizations, they not only hear organization discussion and strategy, they learn about organization members and contributors who may wish to remain anonymous. If these infiltrators rise to leadership positions, as they may be encouraged to do, they may significantly affect the organization's positions, even to the point of becoming full-fledged agents provocateurs.... By rendering law-abiding groups vulnera-

ble to such infiltration, the current FBI guidelines cannot help but make citizens reluctant to join controversial causes or to speak up at organizational gatherings. The emphasis on investigating organizations and not just individuals will also inhibit the formation of political coalitions and large-scale demonstrations.[66]

The FBI's overblown foreign intelligence investigation of a law-abiding domestic organization that opposed United States military aid to El Salvador in the 1980s—the Committee in Solidarity with the People of El Salvador (CISPES)—reveals how insensitive the FBI can be to the exercise of First Amendment rights. During the course of the FBI's surveillance of CISPES, agents "took thousands of photographs at peaceful demonstrations..., surveilled churches and church groups, sent an informant to numerous meetings, rummaged through trash, collected mailing lists, took license plate numbers of vehicles parked outside public meetings, and obtained long distance telephone billing records from telephone companies."[67] Through the use of informants, the FBI gathered information on the political activities of approximately 2,375 individuals and 1,330 organizations, and initiated 178 related investigations that appear to have been based on political ideology rather than on suspicion of criminal activity.[68] Yet this massive government intrusion into the lives of thousands of lawful political activists failed to yield a single criminal charge, let alone a criminal conviction.[69]

Over the past few years, the anti-globalization movement—which first caught the world's attention in 1999 with a 40,000-strong demonstration in Seattle against the World Trade Organization, and which includes non-violent civil disobedience in its repertoire of protest tools—has become the subject of intrusive and disruptive government surveillance and infiltration.[70]

Although the Levi and Smith guidelines were designed to protect us from the kind of FBI misconduct documented by the Church Committee, they failed to safeguard us fully against politically motivated investigations of lawful protest activities. The new Ashcroft guidelines place even fewer restraints on the FBI than did the Smith guidelines. The Ashcroft guidelines threaten to return us to the COINTEL-PRO era when the FBI routinely conducted surveillance without suspicion of criminal conduct, targeted groups for infiltration and disruption based on their ideology, and maintained dossiers on thousands of law-abiding citizens who had expressed political views of which the government disapproved.

III. TARGETING PERCEIVED ENEMIES FOR DETENTION AND DEPORTATION

A. THE AMERICAN CIVIL WAR

At the start of the Civil War in April 1861, President Abraham Lincoln unilaterally suspended the writ of habeas corpus. As a result, tens of thousands of civilians suspected of being disloyal to the Union cause were detained by the military without charge. Despite President Lincoln's action, one such civilian, John Merryman, succeeded in attaining a writ of habeas corpus ordering his release from prison. However, the general responsible for his detention refused to honor the writ, and Merryman's case was reviewed by Chief Justice Roger Taney, sitting in his capacity as a federal circuit judge. Chief Justice Taney held, in a controversial opinion issued later that year, that the Constitution granted the power to suspend the writ only to Congress, thus declaring President Lincoln's actions unconstitutional.[71] While Lincoln largely ignored this lower court opinion, Congress responded by passing the Habeas Corpus Act of 1863, which had the effect of validating Lincoln's suspension of the writ of habeas corpus.

Not until the close of the Civil War, in *Ex Parte Milligan*, did the Supreme Court impose limits on the government's wartime powers. Lambden P. Milligan was a civilian who had been sentenced to death by a military court in Indiana for conspiring to seize munitions from federal arsenals and free Confederate prisoners. In a landmark ruling, the Court overturned his conviction, holding that military tribunals could not take the place of civilian courts in areas where civilian courts were available and in operation.[72] Since Indiana's court system had remained intact during the war, the Court held that Indiana's civilians could not be tried in military tribunals. The Court went on to declare the Constitution "a law for rulers and people, equally in times of war and peace" that "covers with the shield of its protection all classes of men, at all times, and under all circumstances."[73]

B. THE PALMER RAIDS OF WORLD WAR I

The ruling in *Ex Parte Milligan* had long been forgotten by the time the nation next found itself in a state of crisis. During the Red Scare of the World War I era, the fear that communism would spread from Bolshevik Russia to Europe and the United States fueled government investigations of suspected radical dissidents. When the home of Attorney General A. Mitchell Palmer was bombed by anarchists in June 1919, the administration of President Woodrow Wilson interrogated, arrested, and detained as many as ten thousand resident aliens who had been targeted based on their political ideology. Many of the detainees were beaten and forced to sign confessions. These actions, which came to be known as the Palmer Raids, took place in more than thirty cities and resulted in the deportation of more than five hundred immigrants, not one of whom was proved to pose a threat to the United States.[74]

C. THE JAPANESE INTERNMENT OF WORLD WAR II

Following the bombing of Pearl Harbor on December 7, 1941, as the United States entered World War II, President Franklin D. Roosevelt issued Executive Order 9066, which mandated the evacuation, relocation, and internment of the 110,000 men, women, and children of Japanese ancestry then living on the West Coast of the United States.[75] While the government had no evidence that any of these persons—two-thirds of whom were United States citizens— were collaborating with Japan,[76] they were kept in preventive detention under harsh and punishing conditions for much of the war.[77]

Despite the fact that Executive Order 9066 explicitly singled out individuals of Japanese ancestry for preventive detention, the Supreme Court, in *Korematsu v. United States*, refused to strike down the order as a violation of the equal protection clause.[78] The majority of the Court upheld the order as an appropriate wartime measure and affirmed the conviction of Fred Korematsu, a U.S. citizen of Japanese descent, based on his refusal to submit to the internment.[79] But the majority decision was not without its critics. Justice Frank Murphy castigated the government in a bitter dissent:

> Racial discrimination in any form and in any degree has no justifiable part whatever in our democratic way of life. It is unattractive in any setting but it is utterly revolting among a free people who have embraced the principles set forth in the Constitution of the United States. All residents of this nation are kin in some way by blood or culture to a foreign land. Yet they are primarily and necessarily a part of the new and distinct civilization of the United States. They must accordingly be treated at all times as the heirs of the American experiment and as entitled to all the rights and freedoms guaranteed by the Constitution.[80]

In 1984, four decades after the Supreme Court affirmed Korematsu's conviction, a federal district court judge in California set aside the conviction on review of a writ of coram nobis.[81] Judge Marilyn Hall Patel explained in her decision that the government had, "while not confessing error, taken a position tantamount to a confession of error. It has eagerly moved to dismiss without acknowledging any specific reasons for dismissal other than that 'there is no further usefulness to be served by conviction under a statute which has been soundly repudiated.'"[82] Shortly afterward, Congress passed the Civil Liberties Act of 1988, in which it acknowledged the internment's "fundamental injustice" and pledged to "discourage the occurrence of similar injustices and violations of civil liberties in the future."[83] The act extended to each victim of the internment an apology on behalf of the people of the United States and a modest financial reparation.[84]

The Supreme Court has yet to acknowledge that it erred in upholding the constitutionality of Executive Order 9066. In its subsequent decisions interpreting the equal protection clause, however, the Court has held that such race-based classifications must be narrowly tailored to further a compelling governmental interest by the least restrictive means available.[85] One would hope that, under this strict scrutiny test, the Supreme Court would reject the "blanket condemnation of all persons of Japanese descent [in a situation where] no reliable evidence [wa]s cited to show that such individuals were generally disloyal, or had generally so conducted themselves in this area as to constitute a special menace to defense installations or war industries, or had otherwise by their behavior furnished reasonable ground for their exclusion as a group."[86]

Regrettably, the Bush administration has failed to heed the lessons offered by these shameful chapters from our nation's history. Rather than stay true to our constitutional principles during this period of crisis, the administration seems intent on repeating the mistakes of the past.

CHAPTER 2

HOW THE USA PATRIOT ACT UNDERMINES OUR CIVIL LIBERTIES

Just six weeks after the September 11 terrorist attacks on the World Trade Center and the Pentagon, a jittery Congress—exiled from its anthrax-contaminated offices and confronted with warnings that more terrorist assaults were soon to come—capitulated to the Bush administration's demands for an aggressive new arsenal of antiterrorism weapons. Over vigorous objections by civil liberties organizations on both ends of the political spectrum, Congress overwhelmingly approved the USA PATRIOT Act.[1] Along the way, the Republican House leadership, in a display of raw force, jettisoned an antiterrorism bill, unanimously approved by the House Judiciary Committee, that addressed many of the civil liberties concerns raised by the act.[2] In the Senate, the vote in favor of the USA PATRIOT Act was 98 to 1; in the House, the vote was 356 to 66. This hastily drafted, complex, and far-reaching legislation spans 342 pages. Yet it was passed with virtually no public hearing or debate, and it is accompanied by neither a conference report nor a committee report. On October 26, 2001, it was signed into law by a triumphant President George W. Bush.[3]

A number of the USA PATRIOT Act's provisions are uncontroversial. The act nevertheless stands out as radical in the degree to which it sacrifices our political freedoms in the name of national security and consolidates new powers in the executive branch. It achieves these undemocratic ends in at least three ways. First, the act places our First Amendment rights to freedom of speech and political association in jeopardy by creating a broad new crime of "domestic terrorism" and denying entry to noncitizens on the basis of ideology. Second, the act reduces our already low expectations of privacy by granting the government enhanced surveillance powers. Third, the act erodes the due process rights of noncitizens by allowing the government to place them in mandatory detention and deport them from the United States based on political activities that have been recast under the act as terrorist activities.[4]

I. BLURRING THE LINE BETWEEN IDEOLOGY AND TERRORISM

Section 802 of the act creates a federal crime of "domestic terrorism" that broadly extends to "acts dangerous to human life that are a violation of the criminal laws" if they "appear to be intended…to influence the policy of a government by intimidation or coercion," and if they "occur primarily within the territorial jurisdiction of the United States."[5] Because this crime is couched in such vague and expansive terms, it is likely to be read by federal law enforcement agencies as licensing the investigation and surveillance of political activists and organizations that protest government policies, and by prosecutors as licensing the criminalization of legitimate political dissent.[6] Confrontational protest activities, by

Nancy Chang

their very nature, are acts that "appear to be intended...to influence the policy of a government by intimidation or coercion." In addition, clashes between demonstrators and police officers and acts of civil disobedience—even those that do not result in injuries and are entirely nonviolent—could be construed as "dangerous to human life" and in "violation of the criminal laws."

Environmental activists, antiglobalization activists, and antiabortion activists who use direct action to further their political agendas are particularly vulnerable to prosecution as "domestic terrorists." While the equal protection clause bars intentional discrimination on the basis of race or ethnicity, and the First Amendment bars religious and viewpoint-based discrimination, there are grave concerns that the government will use this new crime to target Muslim nationals of Arab and South Asian countries, political activists, and dissident organizations for surveillance, infiltration, and prosecution.

Section 411 of the act poses an ideological test for entry into the United States. Representatives of a political or social group "whose public endorsement of acts of terrorist activity the Secretary of State has determined undermines United States efforts to reduce or eliminate terrorist activities" can no longer enter the country.[7] Entry is also barred to noncitizens who have used their "position of prominence within any country to endorse or espouse terrorist activity," if the secretary of state determines that their speech "undermines United States efforts to reduce or eliminate terrorist activities."[8] Section 411 harkens back to a Cold War–era statute, the McCarran-Walter Act of 1952, which permitted the

Department of State to exclude foreign speakers based on their political beliefs.[9] The act was finally repealed in 1990 amid strong public outcry that it abridged the First Amendment rights of Americans to hear excluded speakers. While it was in place, however, it was used to bar many prominent scholars, writers, and political activists from entering the United States, including Nobel Prize winners Gabriel García Márquez, Pablo Neruda, Dario Fo, Mexican writer and diplomat Carlos Fuentes, and Belgian socialist and writer Ernst Mandel.[10] By permitting the exclusion of aliens based solely on ideological grounds, and by granting the secretary of state virtually unchecked authority in deciding whom to exclude, Section 411 of the USA PATRIOT Act takes us back to the xenophobia of the Cold War.

II. TOLLING THE DEATH KNELL ON PRIVACY

The USA PATRIOT Act launches a three-pronged assault on our privacy. First, the act grants the executive branch unprecedented, and largely unchecked, surveillance powers, including the enhanced ability to track e-mail and Internet usage, conduct sneak-and-peek searches, obtain sensitive personal records from third parties, monitor financial transactions, and conduct nationwide roving wiretaps. Second, the act permits law enforcement agencies to circumvent the Fourth Amendment's requirement of probable cause when conducting wiretaps and searches for a criminal investigation as long as the investigation can be described as having as "a significant purpose" the gathering of foreign intelligence. Third, the act allows for the sharing of information between criminal and intelligence agencies, including grand jury information, and thereby opens the door to a resurgence of domestic spying by the CIA.

The Supreme Court's June 2001 decision in *Kyllo v. United States*[11] serves as a pointed warning that our Fourth Amendment protections are subject to continual erosion by advances in surveillance technologies used by law enforcement agents. The question before the Court in *Kyllo* was whether the use of an advanced thermal detection device that allowed the police to detect the heat emanating from marijuana plants growing inside the defendant's home constituted a "search" for the purposes of the Fourth Amendment. The Court concluded that the use of the device was a search and was presumptively unreasonable without a warrant. In doing so, however, it placed great weight on the fact that the device was new, was "not in general public use," and had been used to "explore details of a private home that would previously have been unknowable without physical intrusion."[12] The Court's decision implies that once a technology is in general public use and its capabilities are known, a reasonable expectation of privacy, which is required in order to receive the protection of the Fourth Amendment, will no longer be found.

Recognizing the serious dangers posed to our privacy by the USA PATRIOT Act's enhanced surveillance procedures, Congress has scheduled a handful of the procedures to expire, or "sunset," on December 31, 2005.[13] However, even these provisions may be employed after the expiration date in the case of foreign intelligence investigations that began before the expiration date and offenses that began or occurred before the sunset date.[14] The Bush administration strenuously objected to the inclusion of the sunset clauses, and if President Bush is reelected, his administration can be expected to exert pressure on Congress to make these provisions permanent.

A. ENHANCED SURVEILLANCE POWERS

To an alarming degree, Congress granted the Bush administration its longstanding wish list of enhanced surveillance tools, coupled with the right to use these tools with only minimal judicial and congressional oversight. In its rush to pass a piece of antiterrorism legislation, Congress failed to exact from the administration, in exchange, a showing that these highly intrusive tools are actually needed to combat terrorism and that the administration can be trusted not to abuse them.

From all outward indications, both the volume of surveillance requests and their scope have increased dramatically since September 11. Surveillance is, of course, secretive by its very nature. Court orders permitting surveillance routinely include a "gag order" that bars the recipient of the court order from disclosing even its existence, while grand jury subpoenas are tightly wrapped in secrecy under Rule 6(e) of the Federal Rules of Criminal Procedure. Although the number of warrants for wiretaps and searches dipped slightly in 2001 from the previous year, for several reasons this dip should not be equated with a decline in surveillance activity.[15] First, warrants issued under the USA PATRIOT Act pack a stronger punch than did their predecessors. The

Nancy Chang

act's provisions enhance the scope of the government's surveillance powers, permit warrants to cover multiple individuals and multiple locations, extend the reach of warrants beyond the geographical limits of the issuing court, and lengthen the life span of many types of warrants. As phrased by Attorney General John Ashcroft, the act, by enhancing the government's surveillance powers, "provides some measures of efficiency that can be of assistance to us."[16] Second, to an increasing degree, requests for third-party records consist of subpoenas and requests for voluntary cooperation that are neither reviewed nor issued by a court.[17] Third, with advances in information technology, a single request for computerized records can easily result in the production of electronic information concerning millions of people.[18]

A recent news account confirms that since the USA PATRIOT Act was passed, law enforcement agencies have been making "unprecedented demands on the telecommunications industry to provide information on [their] subscribers."[19] Albert Gidari, an attorney who represents Internet service providers and telephone companies, has offered that the number "of subpoenas that carriers receive today [for their customer records] is roughly doubling every month," to the point where "we're talking about hundreds of thousands of subpoenas for customer records—stuff that used to require a judge's approval."[20] Peter Swire, a law professor at Ohio State University, has warned that since September 11, law enforcement agencies are exerting pressure on telecommunications companies to turn over customer records voluntarily, in the absence of either a court order or a subpoena, "with the idea that it is unpatriotic if the companies insist too much on legal subpoenas first."[21] Edward Black, the president of the Computer and Communications Industry Association, has similarly warned that law enforcement authorities have been "short-circuiting" regular legal procedures, and that the industry "must be careful not to create a process whereby using a private company somehow empowers the government to do things they cannot legally do under the new laws."[22] According to Jeffrey Eisenach, the president of the Progress and Freedom Foundation, "[C]onsumers should know that information they give to America Online or Microsoft may very well wind up at the IRS or FBI," and that new technologies "will indeed soon give government the ability to monitor the whereabouts of virtually everyone.[23]

Meanwhile, libraries have become "hunting grounds" for FBI agents demanding information on their patrons. Emily Sheketoff, the executive director of the American Library Association, confirms that this "scary" trend has increased with the passage of the USA PATRIOT Act.[24] In addition, the Foreign Intelligence Surveillance Court—which operates largely in secret and rules on government requests to wiretap and search foreign powers and their agents—is increasing its complement of judges from seven to eleven.[25] With the passage of time, we can expect to receive further confirmation that the government is taking full advantage of its enhanced surveillance powers under the USA PATRIOT Act, and that our privacy has been diminished.

Several of the act's enhanced surveillance tools, and the civil liberties concerns they raise, are examined below.

1. SNEAK-AND-PEEK SEARCHES

Section 213 of the USA PATRIOT Act authorizes federal agents to conduct "sneak- and-peek searches," or covert searches of a person's home or office without notice of the execution of the search warrant until after the search has been completed. Section 213 authorizes delayed notice of the execution of a search warrant upon a showing of "reasonable cause to believe that providing immediate notification...may have an adverse result."[26] In addition, Section 213 authorizes the delay of notice of the execution of a warrant to conduct a seizure of items if the court finds a "reasonable necessity" for the seizure.

Sneak-and-peek searches contravene the common-law principle that law enforcement agents must "knock and announce" their arrival before they conduct a search—a requirement that forms an essential part of the Fourth Amendment's reasonableness requirement.[27] In addition, Section 213 contravenes Rule 41(d) of the Federal Rules of Criminal Procedure, which requires that "[t]he officer taking property under the warrant shall give to the person from whom or from whose premises the property was taken a copy of the warrant and a receipt for the property taken or shall leave the copy and receipt at the place from which the property was taken." When notice of a search is delayed, the subject of the search is disadvantaged in several ways. He is foreclosed from pointing out deficiencies in the warrant to the officer executing it. He is also foreclosed from monitoring whether the search is being conducted in accordance with the warrant or the whereabouts of any property removed from his premises pursuant to the warrant.

Under Section 213, notice may be delayed for a "reasonable period." Already, the Department of Justice has staked out its position that a "reasonable period" can be considerably longer than the seven days authorized by the Second Circuit Court of Appeals in *United States v. Villegas*,[28] and by the Ninth Circuit Court of Appeals in *United States v. Freitas*.[29] In its *Field Guidance on New Authorities (Redacted) Enacted in the 2001 Anti-Terrorism Legislation*,[30] the Department states that "[a]nalogy to other statutes suggest [*sic*] that the period of delay could be substantial if circumstances warrant" and cites in support of this proposition a case that found a ninety-day delay in providing notice of a wiretap warrant to constitute "a reasonable time." Notably, Section 213 is not limited to terrorism investigations but extends to all criminal investigations, and it is not scheduled to expire.

2. ACCESS TO RECORDS IN INTERNATIONAL INVESTIGATIONS

Section 215[31] is one of several provisions in the USA PATRIOT Act that lowers the requirements, and extends the reach, of the Foreign Intelligence Surveillance Act of 1978 (FISA).[32] Under Section 215, the director of the FBI or a designee as low in rank as an assistant special agent in charge may apply for a court order requiring the production of "any tangible things (including books, records, papers, documents, and other items)" upon his written statement that these items are being sought for an investigation "to protect against international terrorism or clandestine intelligence activities."[33] A judge presented with an application under Section 215 is required to enter an order if he "finds that the application meets the requirements of this section."[34]

Notably absent from Section 215 is the former FISA restriction that required the government to specify in its application for a court order that "there are specific and articulable facts giving reason to believe that the person to whom the records pertain is a foreign power or an agent of a foreign power."[35] This means that under Section 215, the FBI may obtain sensitive personal records simply by certifying that they are sought for an investigation "to protect against international terrorism or clandestine intelligence activities." The FBI need not suspect the person whose records are being sought of any wrongdoing. Nor is the class of persons whose records are obtainable under Section 215 limited any longer to foreign powers and their agents; it may include U.S. citizens and lawful permanent residents, or "United States persons" in the parlance of the FISA.[36] Although Section 215 bars investigations of United States persons "solely upon the basis of activities protected by the first amendment to the Constitution," it does not bar investigations based on other activities that tie them, no matter how loosely, to an international terrorism investigation.[37]

The FISA provision that was amended by Section 215 had been limited in scope to "records" in the possession of "a common carrier, public accommodation facility, physical storage facility, or vehicle rental facility."[38] But Section 215 contains no limits on the parties from whom the production of tangible things can be required, and it extends beyond "records" to the much larger universe of "tangible things."[39]

A congressional oversight provision requires the attorney general to submit semiannual reports on its activities under Section 215.[40] This section is scheduled to expire on December 31, 2005.

3. TRACKING INTERNET USAGE

Under Section 216 of the act, courts are required to order the installation of a pen register and a trap-and-trace device[41] to track both telephone and Internet "dialing, routing, addressing and signaling information"[42] anywhere within the United States when a government attorney has certified that the information to be obtained is "relevant to an ongoing criminal investigation."[43] Section 216 does not authorize the tracking of the "contents of any wire or electronic communications." In the case of e-mail messages and Internet usage, however, the act does not address the complex question of where to draw the line between "dialing, routing, addressing and signaling information" and "content." Unlike telephone communications, in which the provision of dialing information is separate from, and does not run the risk of revealing content,[44] e-mail messages move together in packets that include both address and content information. Also, Section 216 does not resolve the question of whether a list of Web sites and Web pages that have been visited constitutes "dialing, routing, addressing and signaling information" or "content."

Unfortunately, by providing no guidance on these critical questions, Section 216 gives the government wide latitude to decide what constitutes "content." Of special concern is the fact that Section 216 authorizes the government to install its new Carnivore, or DCS1000, system, a formidable tracking device that is capable of intercepting all forms of Internet activity, including e-mail messages, Web page activity, and Internet telephone communications.[45] Once installed on an Internet service provider (ISP), Carnivore devours *all* of the communications flowing through the ISP's network—not just those of the target of the surveillance but those of all users—tracking not just information but content as well. The FBI claims that through the use of filters, Carnivore "limits the messages viewable by human eyes to those which are strictly included within the court order."[46] However, neither the accuracy of Carnivore's filtering system nor the infallibility of its human programmers has been demonstrated. Although Section 216 requires the government to maintain a record when it utilizes Carnivore, it need not provide the record to the court until thirty days after the termination of the court order authorizing the surveillance.[47] Section 216 is not scheduled to expire.

B. CIRCUMVENTING THE FOURTH AMENDMENT'S PROBABLE CAUSE REQUIREMENT

A letter sent by Assistant Attorney General Daniel J. Bryant of the Department of Justice's Office of Legislative Affairs to key senators shortly after September 11 lays bare the Bush administration's desire to be freed from the Fourth Amendment's imposition of judicial oversight and review of its surveillance activities. In the letter, Bryant brazenly advocated for a suspension of the Fourth Amendment's warrant requirement in situations in which the government is investigating a foreign national security threat:

As Commander-in-Chief, the President *must be able to use whatever means necessary* to prevent attacks upon the United States; this power, by implication, *includes the authority to collect information necessary to its effective exercise*.... The government's interest has changed from merely conducting foreign intelligence surveillance to counter intelligence operations by other nations, to one of preventing terrorist attacks against American citizens and property within the continental United States itself. The courts have observed that even the use of deadly force is reasonable under the Fourth Amendment if used in self-defense or to protect others.... Here, for Fourth Amendment purposes, the right to self-defense is not that of an individual, but that of the nation and its citizens.... *If the government's heightened interest in self-defense justifies the use of deadly force, then it certainly would also justify warrantless searches*.[48]

The Bush administration's efforts to erode the separation of powers doctrine through warrantless searches was given a big assist in Section 218 of the USA PATRIOT Act. This section, which may be the most far-reaching of the surveillance tools introduced by the act, amends FISA's wiretap and physical search provisions. Under FISA, court orders permitting the executive to conduct surreptitious foreign intelligence wiretaps and physical searches may be obtained without the showing of probable cause of criminal conduct demanded by the Fourth Amendment in the case of criminal investigations. Until the enactment of the USA PATRIOT Act, orders to wiretap and conduct searches could not be issued under FISA's lax standards except in situations in which the gathering of *foreign intelligence* information was "*the* purpose" of the surveillance.[49] Under Section 218, however, orders may be issued under FISA's lax standards when the *primary* purpose of the surveillance is *criminal* investigation, as long as the gathering of *foreign intelligence* information can be described as "*a significant* purpose" of the surveillance.[50]

In the seminal case of *United States v. United States District Court for the Eastern District of Michigan (Keith)*,[51] the Supreme Court rejected President Richard Nixon's ambitious bid for the power to conduct warrantless wiretaps when investigating national security threats posed by *domestic* groups with no foreign ties. The Court recognized that national security cases reflect "a convergence of First and Fourth Amendment values not present in cases of 'ordinary' crime."[52] With respect to the First Amendment, the Court wisely observed that "[o]fficial surveillance, whether its purpose be criminal investigation or ongoing intelligence gathering, risks infringement of constitutionally protected privacy of speech" because of "the inherent vagueness of the domestic security concept...and the temptation to utilize such surveillances to oversee political dissent."[53]

The *Keith* Court acknowledged a constitutional basis for the president's domestic security role but refused to exempt the president from the Fourth Amendment's warrant requirement.[54] The Court explained that the oversight function assumed by the judiciary in its review of applications for warrants "accords with our basic constitutional doctrine that individual freedoms will best be preserved through a separation of powers and division of functions among the different branches and levels of Government."[55]

Notably, the *Keith* Court declined to examine "the scope of the President's surveillance power with respect to the activities of *foreign* powers, within or without this country."[56] To fill the vacuum left by the *Keith* decision, in 1978 Congress enacted FISA, which is premised on the assumption that Fourth Amendment safeguards are not as critical in foreign intelligence investigations as they are in domestic criminal investigations. FISA wiretaps and searches may be issued as long as the government has probable cause to believe that the target is a foreign power or its agent, even when the government lacks probable cause of criminal conduct. A foreign power is broadly defined to include "a foreign-based political organization not substantially composed of United States persons."[57]

The Supreme Court has yet to rule on FISA's constitutionality. However, both the Fourth and Ninth Circuits have cautioned that applying FISA's lax standards to criminal investigations raises serious Fourth Amendment concerns. In *United States v. Truong Dinh Hung*, the Fourth Circuit held that "the executive should be excused from securing a warrant only when the surveillance is conducted *'primarily' for foreign intelligence reasons*," because "once surveillance becomes *primarily a criminal investigation*, the courts are entirely competent to make the usual probable cause determination, and because, importantly, individual privacy

Nancy Chang

interests come to the fore and government foreign policy concerns recede when the government is primarily attempting to form the basis for a criminal prosecution."[58] In a similar vein, the Ninth Circuit held in *United States v. Johnson* that "the investigation of criminal activity cannot be the primary purpose of [FISA] surveillance" and that "[FISA] is not to be used as an end-run around the Fourth Amendment's prohibition of warrantless searches."[59]

The constitutionality of Section 218 is in considerable doubt. Until the Supreme Court addresses the matter, the government will find itself in a quandary each time it seeks to prosecute a criminal defendant based on evidence that, although properly obtained under the showing required by Section 218, does not meet the probable cause showing required by the Fourth Amendment. Should the government decide to base prosecutions on such evidence, it will run the risk that the evidence will be suppressed under the Fourth Amendment exclusionary rule.[60] Section 218 is scheduled to expire on December 31, 2005.

C. SHARING OF SENSITIVE CRIMINAL AND FOREIGN INTELLIGENCE INFORMATION

Section 203 of the USA PATRIOT Act authorizes the sharing—without judicial supervision—of several categories of foreign intelligence information between officials of the FBI, CIA, INS, and a number of other federal agencies, when receipt of the information will "assist" the official receiving the information "in the performance of his official duties."[61] In addition, Section 203 authorizes the sharing of information that "involves" foreign intelligence or counterintelligence, as well as "information relating to the capabilities, intentions, or activities of foreign governments or elements thereof, foreign organizations, or foreign persons."

Of greatest concern is Subsection (a) of Section 203, which permits the disclosure of grand jury information. A grand jury is a body consisting of up to twenty-three jurors that is charged with considering evidence and deciding whether to issue a criminal indictment. The powers of a grand jury to subpoena records and witnesses are nearly boundless.[62] Grand juries are generally "unrestrained by the technical procedural and evidentiary rules governing the conduct of criminal trials."[63] Grand jury subpoenas "are issued pro forma and in blank" and "[t]he court exercises no prior control whatsoever upon their use."[64] A grand jury witness may be compelled to testify about, and turn over records revealing, the most personal and sensitive of matters without a showing of probable cause, under threat of being jailed for civil or criminal contempt of court.[65] Those witnesses who are less than truthful in their testimony risk being charged with perjury.[66] No judge monitors a grand jury's day-to-day activities, and courts refrain from curtailing the grand jury's inquisitorial powers except in clear cases of abuse.[67] The "psychological pressure of grand jury interrogation" enables the grand jury to pry statements from witnesses that they would not provide to the police.[68]

Grand jury proceedings are subject to strict rules of secrecy in order to encourage witnesses to make "free and untrammeled disclosures."[69] Section 203(a) of the USA PATRIOT Act, on the other hand, allows grand jury materials to be shared with the CIA and officials of other federal agencies without regard to whether the materials bear on terrorist activities and without prior court approval or court supervision of the use of the materials. With Section 203(a), a CIA agent who has the assistance of cooperative law enforcement agents may use grand jury subpoena powers to compel testimony and the production of documents without having to account to the judiciary.

Like Subsection (a) of Section 203, Subsections (b) and (d) permit the broad disclosure of sensitive information to officials of the federal government without judicial supervision. Subsection (b) permits the disclosure of recordings of intercepted telephone and Internet conversations.[70] Subsection (d) permits the disclosure of foreign intelligence obtained as part of a criminal investigation.[71]

Although some additional sharing of information between agencies is appropriate given the nature of the terrorist threats we face, the act fails to protect us from the dangers posed to our political freedoms and our privacy when sensitive personal information is widely shared without court supervision. A cautionary tale can be found in the 1976 report of the Church Committee, which revealed that the FBI and CIA had spied on and maintained dossiers on thousands of law-abiding citizens—from civil rights workers to anti–Vietnam War protestors—who were targeted solely because the government believed that they harbored politically dissident views.[72]

Section 203(a) is not scheduled to expire. Subsections (b) and (d), however, are scheduled to expire on December 31, 2005.

III. STRIPPING NONCITIZENS OF CONSTITUTIONAL PROTECTIONS

The USA PATRIOT Act deprives noncitizens of their due process and First Amendment rights through two mechanisms that operate in tandem. Section 411 greatly expands the class of noncitizens who are subject to deportation on grounds of terrorism through its broad definitions of the terms "terrorist activity," "engage in terrorist activity," and "terrorist organization." At the same time, Section 412 substantially enlarges the authority of the attorney general to place noncitizens he suspects are engaged in terrorist activities in detention while their deportation proceedings are pending.

A. EXPANDING THE CLASS OF NONCITIZENS SUBJECT TO DEPORTATION

Section 411 amends the Immigration and Nationality Act (INA) by expanding the class of noncitizens that may be deported on grounds of participation in terrorist activities.[73] The term "terrorist activity" is commonly understood to be limited to premeditated and politically motivated violence targeted against a civilian population.[74] Section 411, however, stretches the term beyond recognition to encompass any crime that involves the use of a "weapon or dangerous device (other than for mere personal monetary gain)."[75] Under this broad definition, a noncitizen who, for example, grabs a knife or makeshift weapon in the midst of a heat-of-the-moment altercation or in committing a crime of passion may be subject to deportation as a "terrorist."

The term "engage in terrorist activity" has been expanded to include soliciting funds for, soliciting membership for, and providing material support to a "terrorist organization," even when that organization has legitimate political and humanitarian ends and the noncitizen seeks only to support these lawful ends.[76] In such situations, Section 411 permits guilt to be imposed solely on the basis of political associations protected by the First Amendment.[77]

To complicate matters further, the term "terrorist organization" is no longer limited to organizations that have been officially designated as terrorist and as a consequence have had their designations published in the Federal Register for all to see.[78] Instead, Section 411 now includes as "terrorist organizations" groups that have never been designated as terrorist if they are composed of "two or more individuals, whether organized or not," who engage in specified terrorist activities.[79] In situations in which a noncitizen has solicited funds for, solicited membership for, or provided material support to an undesignated "terrorist organization," Section 411 saddles him with the difficult if not impossible burden of "demonstrat[ing] that he did not know, and should not reasonably have known, that the act would further the organization's terrorist activity."[80] Furthermore, although Section 411 prohibits the deportation of a noncitizen on the grounds that he solicited funds for, solicited membership for, or provided material support to a designated "terrorist organization" at a time when the organization was not designated as such, Section 411 does not appear to prohibit the deportation of a noncitizen on the grounds that he solicited funds for, solicited membership for, or provided material support to an undesignated "terrorist organization" *prior* to the enactment of the act.[81]

B. DETENTION AT THE ATTORNEY GENERAL'S DECREE

At the same time that Section 411 expands the class of noncitizens who are deportable on grounds of terrorism, Section 412 inflates the attorney general's power to detain noncitizens who are suspected of terrorism.[82] Upon no more than the attorney general's unreviewed certification that he has "reasonable grounds to believe" that a noncitizen is engaged in terrorist activities or other activities that threaten the national security, the INS may detain a noncitizen for as long as seven days without charging him with either a criminal or immigration violation.[83] The low level of suspicion that satisfies Section 412 falls far short of the finding of probable cause that would be required to support an arrest under the Fourth Amendment. It more closely approximates the "reasonable and articulable suspicion" that supports no more than a brief investigatory stop.[84]

Furthermore, a noncitizen certified as a terrorist who is charged with an immigration violation—even a technical violation that is unrelated to terrorist activity—is subject to mandatory detention without release on bond until either he is deported from the United States or the attorney general determines that he should no longer be certified as a terrorist.[85] While his immigration proceedings are pending, the attorney general is required to review his certification once every six months.[86] However, Section 412 does not direct the attorney general to notify the noncitizen of the evidence on which the certification is based, or to provide him with an opportunity to contest that evidence, either at an immigration judge hearing or through another administrative review procedure.

Instead, the noncitizen's only available option for seeking review of the attorney general's certification is to file a habeas corpus proceeding in a federal district court seeking his release from detention.[87] At this early stage, the question of what issues the courts will agree to review in habeas proceedings challenging detentions under Section 412 is far from clear. The INS can be expected to argue that the habeas review under Section 412 is restricted to the narrow question of whether the attorney general had "reasonable grounds to believe" that a noncitizen was engaged in terrorist activities or other activities that threaten the national security. But hopefully the courts will agree to examine the underlying questions of whether Section 412 is constitutional in permitting a noncitizen to be held in mandatory detention based on no more than a certification by the attorney general,[88] and whether Section 412 is constitutional to the extent that it permits the attorney general to keep secret from the noncitizen the evidence on which the certification is based.[89]

The Supreme Court has held both immigration proceedings and habeas proceedings to be civil rather than criminal in nature, notwithstanding the fact that deportation is a "drastic measure and at times the equivalent of banishment or exile."[90] Because the Sixth Amendment extends only to criminal proceedings, the government has no obligation to provide noncitizens with free legal counsel in immigration proceedings or in habeas proceedings related to INS detention. As a practical matter, the cost of hiring a lawyer to litigate a habeas proceeding in federal district court, and to appeal the decision to the court of appeals in Washington,

D.C., the court granted exclusive jurisdiction over such appeals by statute, will prove prohibitively expensive for non-citizens in detention under Section 412. The number of attorneys available to provide legal representation to such non-citizens without charge is inadequate to meet the demand.

Even when a noncitizen who is found deportable is eligible for asylum or other relief from deportation, Section 412 does not permit his release.[91] Furthermore, in the event that a noncitizen is found deportable but deportation is "unlikely in the reasonably foreseeable future," he may be detained for an additional period of six months "if the release of the alien will threaten the national security of the United States or the safety of the community or any person."[92] The only review permitted in this situation is habeas review.[93]

It remains to be seen how the executive will wield its new authority under the USA PATRIOT Act. If, however, the months that have elapsed since September 11 serve as a guide, we should brace ourselves for a flagrant disregard of the rule of law by those charged with its enforcement.

CHAPTER 3

EDGING TOWARD GOVERNMENT BY EXECUTIVE FIAT

The Bush administration has not been content simply to wield its new authority under the USA PATRIOT Act. As an adjunct to its military operations abroad, the administration has waged a shadow war at home that has targeted, almost exclusively, Muslim nationals from Arab and South Asian countries. With little concern for the rule of law, the government has interrogated without suspicion, arrested without charge, and detained without justification numerous individuals who are not involved in terrorist activities but who match this religious and ethnic profile. Many detainees have been held virtually incommunicado for weeks and even months without access to those who could assist them in securing their release—their families and friends, attorneys, and consular officials. And as the wall of secrecy the government has erected around the detentions starts to erode, it has become clear that many detainees have been forced to endure harsh and punishing conditions of confinement. Reports of severe physical and psychological abuse at the hands of prison guards are now all too common.

In the pursuit of its shadow war, the administration has not hesitated to grant itself, by executive fiat, "authorization" designed to impart a veneer of legitimacy to its actions.[1] Freshly minted rules permit the INS to detain noncitizens indefinitely without charge, exclude the press and the public from immigration hearings of detainees of special interest, automatically override immigration judges' decisions ordering the release of detainees on bond, withhold the names of detainees, and subject noncitizens and their representatives to protective orders barring them from disclosing what took place at their immigration hearings. In addition, the Department of Justice may now monitor privileged communications between federal inmates and their attorneys without judicial authorization. Citing "exigent circumstances," the Bush administration has put these rules into effect immediately as "interim rules," circumventing procedural safeguards in the Administrative Procedure Act that require agencies to provide the public with notice of new rules and an opportunity to comment on the rules in advance of their implementation.[2]

Yet, for all of the havoc that its investigation of the September 11 attacks has wreaked on the lives of individuals who share little more in common with the hijackers than religion and nationality, the administration has issued only one criminal indictment directly relating to the attacks. And that indictment was issued against Zacarias Moussaoui, the suspected Al Qaeda member who was arrested in August 2001, after flight school personnel in Minnesota became suspicious when he wished to learn how to fly a jetliner without knowing how to take off or land.[3]

By June 2002, well over a dozen lawsuits had been filed challenging various aspects of the government's investigation, and the trial court judges in four of these lawsuits had ruled that the administration had placed itself above the law. Given the strong inclination of the judiciary to defer to the executive in times of crisis, these opinions stand as a testament to the magnitude of executive overreaching in the months since September 11.

I. AMERICA'S DISAPPEARED

Within hours of the terrorist strikes on the World Trade Center and the Pentagon, the FBI, working in close cooperation with the INS and local law enforcement agencies across the country, embarked on a dragnet for suspected terrorists. In its first few days, 75 individuals were rounded up, interrogated, and detained.[4] By November 5, 2001—the last date on which the Bush administration released a cumulative total—the number of detainees had soared to 1,147.[5] In April 2002, one expert estimated that the total had exceeded 2,000.[6]

The administration has been no more forthcoming about the length of time it has held detainees than it has been about the cumulative number of detainees. However, in response to a lawsuit filed under the Freedom of Information Act,[7] it reported on January 11, 2002—three months after the start of its investigation—that 460 individuals remained in INS custody.[8] In February and April 2002, it reported that over 300 individuals remained in INS custody.[9] And on May 29, 2002, it reported that 104 individuals remained in custody.[10]

A. THE RETURN OF PREVENTIVE DETENTION

The government's detention of such large numbers of individuals could, in theory, stand as a measure of its success in identifying and rooting out terrorists within the United States. Unfortunately, a number of factors suggest instead that the government is engaging in preventive detention—a now universally condemned practice that the United States last employed, with disastrous results, when it interned 110,000 people of Japanese descent following the invasion of Pearl Harbor. Under the Fourth Amendment, the government may detain a person accused of a crime only on a showing of probable cause that the person has engaged in criminal conduct. Under the due process clause, a person who has not been accused of a crime has a fundamental right to freedom from bodily restraint. The due process clause requires that a noncitizen who has been charged with an immigration violation but not with a crime be released from detention on bond unless he is shown to pose either a danger to security or a flight risk.[11]

In the nine months following the September 11 attacks, not a single indictment was filed relating to them other than the one filed against Zacarias Moussaoui. The government has not responded to requests to release the number of individuals who have been held under a federal material witness law that permits the government, upon obtaining a court order, to detain an individual whose testimony is material to a criminal proceeding until such time as his testimony is secured. The material witness statute "carve[s] out a carefully limited exception to the general rule that an individual's liberty may not be encroached upon unless there is probable cause to believe that he or she has committed a crime."[12] The number of material witnesses is approximately twenty-six, and it is far from clear how many, if any, of them actually have material information relating to terrorist activities.[13]

The remaining detainees appear to have no links to terrorism. The circumstances of their arrests strongly suggest that they were targeted based on their Middle Eastern appearance and not on individualized suspicion of criminal activity. Nearly all were arrested when visa irregularities were discovered by law enforcement officers who had asked—based on their appearance or reports from suspicious neighbors or acquaintances—to see their immigration papers.[14] In one case, a Moroccan youth was arrested and detained for four months as he sought to enroll in high school when a guidance counselor reported to the police that his tourist visa had expired.[15] In another case, a man from Jordan was arrested and detained as he was seeking to renew his driver's license.[16] In a third case, an Egyptian man was arrested when a police officer he had flagged down to ask for directions asked to see his passport.[17]

Even the Department of Justice has acknowledged that "most of the people arrested in the weeks after the terror attacks have since been cleared of any connection to the attacks or terror groups."[18] And the department's six-month report to Congress on the INS's compliance with Section 412 of the USA PATRIOT Act,[19] which provides for the mandatory detention of suspected alien terrorists, establishes that the attorney general has yet to certify a single noncitizen as a terrorist under the act.[20] As Representative John Conyers Jr.—who, as the ranking minority member of the House Judiciary Committee, led the fight in the House in opposition to the USA PATRIOT Act—remarked, "The entire justification for Attorney General Ashcroft's dragnet approach to detaining Arab and Muslim Americans has collapsed with this admission that he hasn't been able to identify a single terrorist."[21]

In addition, Ashcroft has made no secret of his view that the current crisis empowers the INS to keep any noncitizen of special interest in preventive detention for as long as it takes the FBI to complete an investigation of that person and either criminally indict him or clear him for release from detention. On September 17, 2001, Ashcroft announced an astounding new interim rule authorizing the INS to detain aliens without charge for forty-eight hours or, in the event of an "emergency or other extraordinary circumstance," for an uncapped "reasonable period of time."[22] In the past, the INS was authorized to detain aliens without charge for only twenty-four hours. By authorizing the arbitrary and potentially indefinite detention of noncitizens, the new rule ignores the Supreme Court's recent ruling in *Zadvydas v. Davis* that the protections of the due process clause extend to "all persons" in the United States, including deportable noncitizens.[23] In addition, it violates Section 412 of the USA PATRIOT Act, which precludes the attorney general from detaining for more than seven days without charge noncitizens whom he has certified that he has "reasonable grounds to believe" are engaged in terrorist activities or other activities that threaten the national security."[24]

Documents produced in response to a lawsuit filed under the Freedom of Information Act illustrate Ashcroft's scorn for the rights of INS detainees under the due process clause to prompt and meaningful notice of the charges on which they are being held and an opportunity to rebut those charges.[25] Of the 718 cases for which relevant information was provided, in 317 cases immigration charges were brought more than forty-eight hours after arrest, and in 36 cases charges were brought 28 days or more after arrest.[26] More disturbing yet, in 13 cases charges were brought more than 40 days after arrest; and in 9 cases charges were brought more than 50 days after arrest.[27] One Saudi Arabian national was detained for 119 days before being charged.[28]

Ashcroft has also declared that he will resort to any pretext to keep individuals of special interest in preventive detention, including minor immigration violations that ordinarily would not result in detention. In a speech to the nation's mayors, Ashcroft stated:

> Robert Kennedy's Justice Department, it is said, would arrest mobsters for "spitting on the sidewalk" if it would help in the battle against organized crime. It has been and will be the policy of this Department of Justice to use the same aggressive arrest and detention tactics in the war on terror.
> Let the terrorists among us be warned: If you overstay your visa—even by one day—we will arrest you. If you violate a local law, you will be put in jail and kept in custody as long as possible. We will use every available statute. We will seek every prosecu-

torial advantage. We will use all our weapons within the law and under the Constitution to protect life and enhance security for America.[29]

Ashcroft has made good on his threat. Lucas Guttentag, director of the American Civil Liberties Union's Immigrant Rights Project, has explained, "Generally in the past, when immigration violations like overstaying your visa or working without authorization were enforced, it was without detention. Usually no bond was required, and anyone who agreed to leave the country voluntarily was allowed to leave promptly. Now there is strict enforcement in a selective and discriminatory way against people from the Middle East who are denied bond and detained for lengthy periods, even after they've agreed to leave."[30]

In late October 2001, the Department of Justice issued an unprecedented interim rule that grants a district director—a mid-level INS employee who plays a prosecutorial function in immigration proceedings—the authority to continue the preventive detention of a noncitizen even though an immigration judge, who is a neutral decision maker, has ordered his release on bond. The noncitizen may be held for as long as it takes the Board of Immigration Appeals to review the immigration judge's order—a period that can last for months.[31] This new automatic override rule may be applied whenever a district director has set bond at ten thousand dollars or higher, without regard to the nature of the underlying immigration violation. In short, the rule allows a solitary unelected official to deprive a noncitizen who stands accused of a minor immigration violation of his fundamental right to freedom, possibly for months, even though an impartial immigration judge has found, based on the evidence presented at a formal administrative hearing, that the noncitizen poses neither a danger to security nor a flight risk. In doing so, the rule vests the powers of prosecutor, judge, and jury in a single government bureaucrat—a stark violation of the Constitution's separation of powers.

Even after noncitizens have been ordered to leave the United States and are ready to do so, they are often kept in preventive detention by the INS for the weeks, or even months, that it takes the FBI to clear them of ties to terrorism.[32] As of February 2002, the INS was blocking the departures of eighty-seven noncitizens who were awaiting FBI clearance.[33] Most of these detainees were Arab or Muslim, and many had spent more than a hundred days in prison waiting to leave the country.[34] A class action lawsuit filed by the Center for Constitutional Rights in April 2002 on behalf of this group charges that the government has tossed out the Bill of Rights by presuming these detainees guilty until investigation proves them innocent.[35] The complaint in this suit, *Turkmen v. Ashcroft*, alleges that the detentions violate the due process clause, which bars the INS from depriving a noncitizen of his liberty except when a legitimate immigration purpose is served. Continued detention beyond the time necessary to deport a noncitizen serves no such purpose. The complaint further alleges that the detentions violate the Fourth Amendment, which requires the government to formally charge suspects with a crime and provide them with a probable cause hearing before a neutral magistrate within forty-eight hours of arrest.[36] The government has not only failed to provide these Fourth Amendment protections to the detainees, it has failed to provide the detainees with the other procedural safeguards guaranteed by the Constitution to criminal defendants, including the right under the Fifth Amendment to a Miranda warning prior to custodial detention, and the rights under the Sixth Amendment to counsel at the government's expense and to a speedy trial. The suit also raises international law claims. No court rulings have been issued in the *Turkmen* suit as of the date of publication.

Furthermore, the government has overreached in its use of the federal material witness statute, which authorizes the detention of an individual whose testimony is material to a criminal proceeding, by applying it in situations where a criminal proceeding has yet to be commenced and only a grand jury investigation is pending. Judge Shira Scheindlin of the Manhattan federal district court ruled on April 30, 2002, that the government had pushed the material witness statute beyond its limits when it detained Osama Awadallah, a student who knew two of the September 11 hijackers, for the sole purpose of securing his testimony before a grand jury.[37] In a carefully reasoned and meticulously detailed opinion that spans sixty pages, Judge Scheindlin explained:

> If the government has probable cause to believe a person has committed a crime, it may arrest that person. Indeed, if the government suspects a person may have committed a crime, regardless of the reasons that motivate that suspicion, it may use all of

its resources to confirm that suspicion by gathering evidence to establish probable cause that the person committed a crime.

But since 1789, no Congress has granted the government the authority to imprison an innocent person in order to guarantee that he will testify before a grand jury conducting a criminal investigation. A proper respect for the laws that Congress does enact—as well as the inalienable right to liberty—prohibits this Court from rewriting the law, no matter how exigent the circumstances.[38]

Ashcroft has criticized Judge Sheindlin's ruling, and the Department of Justice has filed papers preserving the government's right to appeal the ruling to the Second Circuit Court of Appeals.[39]

B. A WALL OF GOVERNMENT SECRECY

Given the profoundly disturbing legal problems presented by the preventive detention of as many as two thousand individuals who have no links to terrorism but have been singled out because of their religion and nationality, it is no surprise that the Bush administration has gone to great lengths to shroud the detentions in secrecy.

1. BLOCKING ACCESS BETWEEN DETAINEES AND THE OUTSIDE WORLD

In the weeks and months following September 11, the families, friends, and attorneys of those placed in detention encountered one roadblock after another as they frantically sought to locate detainees and assist them in securing their release.[40] Government officials rebuffed requests for information concerning the whereabouts of detainees, and detainees were limited to one telephone call per week or, in some cases, per month.[41] To make matters worse, many detainees were transferred between prisons, and their families, friends, and attorneys were not provided with notice of these transfers.[42] Even when detainees were located, family members were often denied permission to visit.[43]

These efforts to block communications between the INS detainees and the outside world have, among other things, blocked access to counsel. Unlike criminal defendants, who are entitled under the Sixth Amendment to a state-funded attorney, individuals facing immigration charges must retain counsel on their own. Many INS detainees were frustrated in doing so by prison restrictions on telephone access and by the unavailability of accurate contact information for providers of legal services.[44] Equally troubling is the report of Amnesty International that some of the people being detained may not have been "advised of their right to an attorney during their initial period in custody, when many were questioned by the FBI before being handed over to the INS," and that "some detainees' requests to contact an attorney were denied during initial questioning, contrary to both U.S. law and international standards."[45]

Government efforts to block communications between INS detainees and the outside world have also caused many detainees to accede to requests from their interrogators that they sign forms waiving their rights to counsel and to notification of consular officials from their countries of origin under the Vienna Convention, to contest the immigration charges filed against them, and to seek release on bond.[46] Without the benefit of legal advice, disadvantaged by language barriers, and confronted by harsh prison conditions and hostile interrogation, many detainees concluded that their best option was to agree to leave the United States without putting up a fight.[47]

2. KEEPING THE IDENTITIES OF DETAINEES SECRET

As difficult as it has been for family members, friends, and attorneys to locate and assist individual detainees, it has been even more difficult for organizations concerned with the welfare of the detainees as a group to determine who has been detained, much less what has happened to them and what their needs are. The government has provided only minimal information concerning the detainees, and it has steadfastly refused to reveal the identities of detainees held by the INS and as material witnesses. Two lawsuits seeking this information have been filed by concerned organizations.

The first lawsuit, *CNSS v. Ashcroft*, was filed under the federal Freedom of Information Act and seeks, for the entire universe of September 11 detainees, the detainee's name, citizenship status, and location, along with the dates of his arrest and release, the dates on which charges were filed, and the nature and disposition of the charges.[48] The *CNSS* suit was filed in December 2001 and is pending in the federal district court in Washington, D.C. The plaintiffs include more than twenty civil liberties and human rights organizations.

The government has asserted in response to the *CNSS* suit, as well as other suits, that releasing the names of INS detainees and material witness detainees—even those who have been cleared of ties to terrorism—could harm its investigation because terrorist groups might be able to fit information that appears innocuous into a larger "mosaic" and use the information to thwart the government's antiterrorism efforts.[49] In addition, the government has asserted that releasing the names of the detainees could harm their reputations.[50]

The *CNSS* plaintiffs argue that the government's refusal to release the names of detainees who are not linked to terrorism serves no national security purpose and that the government's mosaic theory is merely a screen to hide misconduct.[51] By now, terrorist groups surely have been able to determine which, if any, of their members have been detained. Furthermore, given the extensive evidence that the government has abused its powers with respect to the detainees, the public interest in knowing their names is compelling.[52] In addition, the plaintiffs have characterized the government's solicitude for the privacy interests of the detainees as "suspect, as it is the government that continues to associate the detainees with terrorism and it is the government that claims 'it cannot rule out' links to terrorism, even while admitting that it has no evidence to that effect."[53] As the plaintiffs point out, "[I]f the government were truly concerned about protecting the detainees from stigmatization, it could announce that none or only a few of them have actually been linked to terrorism."[54] The court has not yet ruled on the merits of this lawsuit.

The second lawsuit, *New Jersey American Civil Liberties Union v. County of Hudson*, was filed in January 2002 under the New Jersey Right to Know Law and seeks similar information concerning the subset of September 11 detainees who have been housed in two New Jersey prisons, the Hudson County Correctional Center and the Passaic County Jail.[55] In a March 26, 2002, opinion delivered from the bench, Judge Arthur D'Italia described secret detentions as "odious to a democratic society," explaining that "[n]othing is easier for the government to assert than the disclosure of the arrest of X would jeopardize investigation Y," and ordered the state prisons to release the requested information.[56] The government has obtained a stay of Judge D'Italia's order while its appeal is under consideration, and no names have been released thus far.[57] The INS has also issued an interim rule that seeks to override the New Jersey State Right to Know Law by prohibiting state and local officials from releasing the names of federal detainees housed in their facilities.[58]

3. BARRING THE PRESS AND PUBLIC FROM IMMIGRATION JUDGE HEARINGS

Under a directive issued to immigration judges on September 21, 2001, by Chief Immigration Judge Michael Creppy, immigration hearings in cases determined to be of special interest to the September 11 investigation have been closed in their entirety to all members of the press and public.[59] In addition, under the directive, special interest cases cannot be listed on the calendar of scheduled hearings, and immigration court personnel can neither confirm nor deny their existence. The directive applies without regard to whether the matters covered in the hearing are sensitive or mundane.

The Creppy directive runs counter to a long and unbroken

tradition of openness in immigration hearings.[60] For nearly fifty years, INS regulations have presumed that the press and public are welcome to attend hearings except in those limited circumstances in which an immigration judge has made an individualized determination that a hearing, or portions of a hearing, should be closed in order to protect witnesses, parties, or the public interest.[61] The directive also runs counter to case law establishing that under the First Amendment, members of the press and public have an interest in attending government proceedings, while under the due process clause, individuals whose rights are to be decided by such proceedings have an interest in open proceedings. These cases recognize that press and public scrutiny of government proceedings encourages honesty, candor, and impartiality on the part of their participants, while allowing the public to witness for itself whether justice has been done.[62]

In two separate lawsuits brought by media plaintiffs—one in Newark, New Jersey, and the other in Detroit, Michigan—two federal district court judges have recently issued preliminary injunctions enjoining the government's use of the Creppy directive on First Amendment grounds.[63] On May 19, 2002, Chief Judge John Bissell issued a preliminary injunction in *North Jersey Media Group v. Ashcroft* enjoining the operation of the Creppy directive on the grounds that it was not narrowly tailored to serve the interests asserted by the government and therefore could not withstand the strong presumption of access to government proceedings under the First Amendment.[64] As Judge Bissell observed, nothing in the Creppy directive prohibits the detainee or his lawyer from disclosing any information the government seeks to conceal.[65] Judge Bissell also observed that to the extent government claims that the Creppy directive "serve[s] the interest of insulating the individual detainee from humiliation or stigma, its mandates sweep too broadly because it does not permit the individual to elect such protective treatment."[66] Judge Bissell noted that although some detainees wish to have their hearings closed, others may view closure of their hearings as having "a negative impact upon them and their interests."[67] Judge Bissell suggested that a more narrowly tailored way to address the government's concerns would be to close hearings at those times, if any, when sensitive evidence is disclosed.[68]

Judge Nancy Edmunds reached similar conclusions in her April 3, 2002, opinion in *Detroit Free Press v. Ashcroft*. Judge Edmunds issued a preliminary injunction permitting the media plaintiffs in the case to attend the immigration proceedings of September 11 detainee Rabih Haddad. In doing so, Judge Edmunds explained the important First Amendment values served by open access to Haddad's proceedings:

> Haddad's right to remain in the United States will be decided at these proceedings. It is important for the public, particularly individuals who feel that they are being targeted by the Government as a result of the terrorist attacks of September 11, to know that even during these sensitive times the Government is adhering to immigration procedures and respecting individuals' rights. Openness is necessary for the public to maintain confidence in the

value and soundness of the Government's actions, as secrecy only breeds suspicion as to why the Government is proceeding against Haddad and aliens like him. And if in fact the Government determines that Haddad is connected to terrorist activity or organizations, a decision made openly concerning his deportation may assure the public that justice has been done.[69]

The government is expected to appeal Judge Bissell's ruling to the Third Circuit Court of Appeals. It has already appealed Judge Edmunds's ruling to the Sixth Circuit. The Sixth Circuit, however, has denied the government's motion for a stay, citing the government's failure to demonstrate a likelihood of success on its claims.[70]

Faced with two lawsuits challenging the constitutionality of the Creppy directive, the Department of Justice issued an interim rule on May 28, 2002, that "complements" the Creppy directive. The new rule allows the INS to close hearings to the press and public and to apply for protective orders preventing noncitizens and their attorneys from disclosing "sensitive law enforcement or national security information" revealed in the hearings.[71] The rule makes an end-run around our nation's strong tradition, rooted in the First Amendment, of openness in governmental proceedings. The rule allows the closing of immigration hearings in their entirety whenever information covered by a protective order is considered, no matter how tangential to the issues at hand. At the same time, the rule instructs immigration judges to give "deference" to law enforcement agents in deciding what is sensitive and establishes that the rule extends to seemingly insignificant details if the government believes that a terrorist organization could piece them together into a mosaic of intelligence gathering.

C. DANGEROUS AND PUNISHING CONDITIONS OF CONFINEMENT

The government's secrecy surrounding the preventive detentions has not only concealed facts suggesting that the detentions are illegal; it has concealed the dangerous and punishing conditions imposed upon the detainees. As the stories of more and more detainees are made known, a gruesome picture has emerged. Untold numbers of detainees with no links to terrorism or records of violence, charged with no more than minor immigration violations, have been placed in solitary confinement for months at a stretch. They have been housed in small windowless cells under bright lights that remain on twenty-four hours a day. They have been deprived of reading materials and other diversions and have been given infrequent opportunities to shower and exercise. Upon leaving their cells, they have been subjected to strip searches and body cavity searches, and they have been placed in "three-piece suits" consisting of leg restraints and a belly chain linked to a set of handcuffs.[72] At the other extreme are detainees who have been housed in overcrowded pens with convicted murderers and other violent criminals.

Reports of ethnic and religious epithets being hurled by prison guards and fellow inmates, along with false accusations of responsibility for the September 11 attacks, appear to be commonplace among September 11 detainees.[73] Two Egyptians reported that the FBI agents who initially interrogated them repeatedly yelled and swore at them.[74] In addition, a number of detainees have been injured at the hands of their prison guards. Syed Amjad Ali Jaffri, a plaintiff in *Turkmen v. Ashcroft*, complained that his face was slammed into walls and kicked by prison guards. His lower front teeth were loosened in the process, and although he was in extreme pain, he was not allowed to see a dentist.[75] While prison guards stood by, a Pakistani man was reportedly beaten by fellow inmates shortly after a newspaper article was circulated in the prison stating that he was under investigation for terrorism.[76] Osama Awadallah reported that during the three weeks he was kept in custody as a material witness, he was repeatedly abused, both physically and verbally, by prison guards.[77] In one incident, he was grabbed by the hair while he was shackled and forced to face an American flag by a prison guard who told him, "This is America."[78]

In addition, a number of detainees have complained that they were not provided with necessary medical treatment.[79] An Iranian man was reported to have suffered a stroke that went untreated for three months while he remained in solitary confinement.[80] And Rafiq Butt, a fifty-five-year-old Pakistani restaurant worker, died of a heart attack in October 2001 while being detained in the Hudson County Correctional Center.[81] Butt was reported to have been picked up based on a tip to the FBI from a pastor of a church near his home, and his only transgression was overstaying his visitor's visa.[82] He had already agreed to leave the United States but had been prevented from doing so because he had not yet been cleared by the FBI.[83] Butt's tragic end shows how preventive detention, secrecy, and acutely stressful conditions of confinement can be a deadly combination.

In short, the government's post–September 11 use of preventive detention has turned the presumption of innocence on its head. As Professor David Cole, a cooperating attorney of the Center for Constitutional Rights, stated, "[I]nstead of presuming someone is innocent until proven guilty, we presume that they're guilty. We lock them up. We then investigate. And once we determine that they're innocent, we release or deport them."[84]

Unfortunately, the "war on terrorism" promises to be a war without end. Four trial court judges have condemned the administration for edging our nation toward government by executive fiat, and we must continue to call upon the judiciary to establish limits on the power of the executive branch during times of national crisis.

II. MONITORING THE ATTORNEY-CLIENT COMMUNICATIONS OF FEDERAL INMATES

In a move that sent shock waves throughout the criminal defense bar, the Bureau of Prisons issued an interim rule on October 31, 2001, that allows the Department of Justice to monitor privileged communications between federal inmates and their attorneys without judicial authorization.[85] This rule is designed to chill, if not freeze, the confidential discussions between an inmate and his attorney that are essential to a well-prepared defense.

Under the new rule, the attorney general may order the

"monitoring or review of communications" between an inmate in the custody of the Bureau of Prisons and his attorneys whenever the attorney general certifies that "reasonable suspicion exists to believe that a particular inmate may use communications with attorneys or their agents to further or facilitate acts of terrorism."[86] The Bureau of Prisons generally must provide the inmate and his attorney with prior written notice of the government's intention to monitor their communications. It need not do so, however, when the Department of Justice has obtained a court order allowing for monitoring without such notice.[87] A "privilege team" consisting of "individuals not involved in the underlying investigation" is required to review monitored communications and to ensure that portions protected by the attorney-client privilege are not retained.[88] The rule provides, however, that communications are not privileged if the Department of Justice finds that they "would facilitate criminal acts or a conspiracy to commit criminal acts" or "are not related to the seeking or providing of legal advice." Unless the privilege team "determines that acts of violence are imminent," it may not disclose privileged material except under a court order.[89] The rule extends not just to convicted criminals but to pretrial detainees, INS detainees, and material witnesses, who are presumed innocent and entitled to greater protection under the Constitution.

The interim rule represents an unprecedented attack on the attorney-client privilege, an evidentiary privilege that traces its roots back to British common law. This privilege protects against the compelled disclosure of confidential communications between attorney and client. The Supreme

Court has explained that "[i]ts purpose is to encourage full and frank communication between attorneys and their clients and thereby promote broader public interests in the observance of law and administration of justice."[90]

Although the courts have recognized a narrow "crime-fraud exception" to the privilege, they have been careful to reserve to a neutral judge the responsibility for determining whether a communication between attorney and client is intended to further criminal activity—the criterion for falling within this exception.[91] Through the new rule, however, the executive branch has unilaterally granted itself the exclusive authority to make these sensitive and highly nuanced determinations. Given the intensely adversarial nature of the relationship between the executive and the inmates in its custody, this authority should remain with the judiciary.

The rule also threatens the attorney-client privilege by turning over to the executive the sole discretion to decide what constitutes "acts of terrorism" and the "facilitation" of such acts; when "reasonable suspicion exists to believe" that an inmate "may use communications" with attorneys to facilitate such acts; when communications "are not related to the seeking or providing of legal advice"; and when "acts of violence are imminent." None of these terms is defined in the rule, and each is susceptible to a sweeping interpretation that would open the door to government monitoring of privileged attorney-client communications. Their vagueness will permit the discriminatory application of the rules on the basis of an inmate's racial, ethnic, religious, and political affiliations.

In the case of inmates who face criminal charges, the rule also interferes with the Sixth Amendment's guarantee of effective assistance of counsel,[92] which at the very least entails the ability to communicate with one's lawyer freely and candidly, without fear of government eavesdropping.[93]

Furthermore, the "safeguards" in the rule are inadequate to protect against the chilling of communications between inmates and their attorneys. The "privilege team" is likely to consist of Department of Justice employees whose over-arching objectives are the same as those of the prosecution team. A lawsuit challenging the rule was filed on May 8, 2002, by Mohamed Rashid Daoud Al'Owhali, who is serving a life sentence in connection with the 1998 bombing of the U.S. Embassy in Nairobi, Kenya.[94] Al'Owhali alleges in his complaint that although the government has not provided notice of an intention to monitor his communications with his attorney, Frederick Cohn, his communications have nevertheless been stifled because "the regulations permit, and [Al'Owhali] is in danger of, monitoring without notice on an *ex parte* application to a judge."

Unfortunately, Al'Owhali's concerns about surreptitious government monitoring of his communications with his attorney are not academic. On April 9, 2002, with much fanfare, Ashcroft announced at a New York City press conference that Lynne Stewart, a civil rights attorney known for her zealous advocacy of controversial clients, had been arrested based on her representation of Sheikh Omar Abdel Rahman.[95] Rahman is the spiritual leader of the Islamic Group, an Egyptian group that has been designated by the secretary of state as a foreign terrorist organization, and he is currently serving a life sentence for conspiring to bomb New York City landmarks. The indictment reveals that the government had been monitoring Stewart's communications with Rahman for several years under a warrant issued by the Foreign Intelligence Surveillance Court, and that its case rests on the monitored communications.[96] Stewart has been charged with providing material support to a designated foreign terrorist organization, a crime that can be punished by a term of fifteen years of imprisonment. Specifically, Stewart is accused of serving as a conduit for the exchange of information between Rahman and others, a charge that Stewart vehemently denies. Stewart was released on a $500,000 personal recognizance bond. In the meantime, her client files and computer files relating to Rahman and other clients have been seized by the FBI.[97] At the press conference announcing Stewart's indictment, Ashcroft also announced that future conversations between Rahman and his attorneys would be monitored under the interim rule.

The issuance of the interim rule, combined with the cautionary tale to be found in the prosecution of Lynne Stewart, sends the clear message that attorneys who represent individuals charged with terrorist crimes now run the risk of landing in jail alongside their clients and having their client files seized by FBI agents.

CHAPTER 4

SILENCING POLITICAL DISSENT

When U.S. national security is threatened, our commitment to the First Amendment and the democratic values it embodies becomes all the more essential. Crises force us to make decisions on the weightiest of matters—whether to declare war, whether to take military action and compel military service, whether to curtail our political and personal freedoms, whom to call friend and whom foe. The specter of casualties—both military and civilian, American and foreign—looms in the balance. Once made, these decisions are certain to carry long-lasting repercussions extending far beyond the geographical confines of the United States.

Public participation in decision making is the hallmark of a democratic society. Open debate that invites the vigorous presentation of opposing viewpoints both enriches our understanding of the problems we face and challenges us to find innovative solutions. Yet, it is precisely at moments like the present, when the national security is under threat, that First Amendment values are most likely to be abandoned in favor of authoritarian rule. With a growing sense of uneasiness, we have witnessed the Bush administration amass enormous new powers in the months since September 11. And we have witnessed the administration, in an effort to maintain a free hand in the exercise of its new powers, employ strategies that are calculated to silence dissent. First, it has questioned the patriotism of those who oppose its policies, thereby fostering a climate of intolerance of dissent. Second, it has sought to discourage political activism by imposing guilt by association. Third, it has restricted access to government information, which has stymied the press, the public, and even Congress in their efforts to hold the executive accountable for its actions.

I. A QUESTION OF PATRIOTISM

The First Amendment, through its guarantee of the freedom of speech, has sustained America's most prized traditions— independence of thought, diversity of opinion, and the right to the uninhibited expression of one's views, no matter how unpopular. In the words of Justice Robert Jackson:

> [F]reedom to differ is not limited to things that do not matter much. That would be a mere shadow of freedom. The test of its substance is the right to differ as to things that touch the heart of the existing order. If there is any fixed star in our constellation, it is that no official, high or petty, can prescribe what shall be orthodox in politics, nationalism, religion, or other matters of opinion....[1]

The Bush administration has done violence to these cherished traditions by challenging not simply the ideas but the patriotism of its critics. Shortly after the September 11 attacks, Bill Maher, the host of the television show *Politically Incorrect*, quipped, "We have been the cowards, lobbing cruise missiles from two thousand miles away.... Staying in the airplane when it hits the building—say what you want about that, it's not cowardly."[2] White House Press Secretary Ari Fleischer seized upon Maher's statement and angrily warned that Americans "need to watch what they say," and that "this is not a time for remarks like that."[3]

More ominous yet was the warning of Attorney General Ashcroft, who, as the nation's top law enforcement officer, heads the Department of Justice and all of its divisions, including the FBI, the INS, the Bureau of Prisons, and the U.S. Attorneys. Testifying before the Senate Committee on the Judiciary in December 2001, Ashcroft admonished that "those who scare peace-loving people with phantoms of lost liberty...your tactics only aid terrorists, for they erode our national unity and diminish our resolve," and "[t]hey give ammunition to America's enemies and pause to America's friends."[4]

The administration's willful refusal to recognize the distinction between core political speech, which enjoys the full protection of the First Amendment, and the crime of treason, has produced an environment in which those who question the soundness of our government's response to the events of September 11 have been faced with visits from the FBI, death threats, and other adverse consequences.[5]

A. THOUGHT POLICE

The initiation of FBI investigations of law-abiding Americans based on tips that they hold controversial views

94

has become all too common since September 11. On October 23, 2001, shortly after a sixty-year-old retiree in San Francisco, Barry Reingold, complained at his local gym, "This war is not just about getting terrorists[, i]t's also about money and corporate oil profits," FBI agents arrived at his home to question him about his political views.[6] On October 26, 2001, FBI agents turned up at the home of A. J. Brown, a college freshman in North Carolina, to investigate a report of an "un-American poster" on display in her home. As it turned out, the poster in question criticized President Bush's support for the death penalty during his tenure as the governor of Texas.[7] Before leaving, the agents let Brown know that their investigation had already uncovered the fact that her mother was in the armed forces, and they asked Brown if she had any pro-Taliban materials.[8]

FBI agents even paid a visit to the Art Car Museum in Houston, Texas, based on a tip that "there was some material or artwork that was of a threatening nature to the President."[9] On November 7, 2001, the agents spent an hour examining the gallery's exhibit, "Secret Wars," which included a number of antiwar pieces commissioned before September 11, and questioning the docent as to who the artists were, how the gallery was funded, and who had visited the exhibit.[10]

These recent incidents recall a pair of Supreme Court cases—one decided during the presidency of Lyndon Baines Johnson, and the other decided during the presidency of Ronald Reagan. Each case involved a law-abiding citizen whose life was turned upside down as a consequence of his having made an intemperate remark that was construed by a law enforcement agency as a threat against the life of the president of the United States. At issue in the first case was a remark made in 1966 during a rally against the Vietnam War on the grounds of the Washington Monument. Eighteen-year-old Robert Watts was overheard by an investigator for the Army Counter Intelligence Corps as saying, "They always holler at us to get an education. And now I have already received my draft classification as 1-A and I have got to report for my physical this Monday coming. I am not going. If they ever make me carry a rifle the first man I want to get in my sights is L.B.J."[11] On the basis of this statement, Watts was convicted under a 1917 statute that makes it a felony to "knowingly and willfully...[make] any threat to take the life of...or to inflict bodily harm upon the President of the United States...."[12] At issue in the second case was a remark made on March 30, 1981, the date of an attempt on the life of President Reagan.[13] In a spontaneous conversation with a coworker, Ardith McPherson, a clerical employee in a county constable's office, stated, "[S]hoot, if they go for him again, I hope they get him."[14] McPherson's remark was overheard and reported to the constable, who fired her.[15]

By examining the contexts in which these remarks were made, the Supreme Court properly identified them as heated political commentary entitled to the full protection of the First Amendment, and not as actual threats against the life of a president. On this basis, the Court overturned Watts's felony conviction and ordered McPherson's reinstatement to her job. These cases represent a positive development in First Amendment jurisprudence, but at the same time they illustrate how eager law enforcement agencies are to read sinister meanings into innocent remarks that display an irreverent attitude toward authority.

The Department of Justice has initiated two programs since September 11, and it is about to initiate a third, that are likely to unleash a flood of spurious tips from overanxious neighbors, acquaintances, grudge-bearing coworkers, and jilted lovers concerning individuals who have expressed their opposition to the government's antiterrorism measures. In January 2002, the Department of Justice widely distributed a preparedness guide urging citizens to listen for reports "of someone who...claims membership in a terrorist organization" and "take what you hear seriously," and to report "patterns of suspicious activity" to the FBI.[16] In March 2002, Ashcroft unveiled plans to increase the budget of the Neighborhood Watch Program by nearly two million dollars so that it can expand its surveillance role beyond the detection of neighborhood crimes to the detection of terrorist activity.[17] In August 2002, the Department of Justice is scheduled to launch Operation TIPS, the code name for the Terrorist Information and Prevention System. The initial phase of this nationwide terrorism reporting system will involve one million American workers in ten cities whose ranks will include truckers, mail carriers, train conductors, and utility workers, and who will constitute a formal network for reporting suspected terrorist activities.[18] With gallows humor, Representative Dennis Kucinich of Ohio observed, "It appears we are being transformed from an information society to an informant society. Do the math. One tip a day per person and within a year the whole country will be turned in, and we can put up a big fence around the country and we'll be safe."[19]

1. LOCKSTEP NATION

The Bush administration's intolerance of political views not in lockstep with its own has fueled public intolerance of dissent. While the First Amendment applies only to the government, its values are eroded whenever intolerance silences alternative views.

On September 14, 2001, Congress granted President Bush broad and open-ended authority under the War Powers Act to use force, not only against nations but against any "organizations, or persons he determines planned, authorized, committed, or aided the terrorist attacks that occurred on September 11, 2001, or harbored such organizations or persons, in order to prevent any future acts of international terrorism against the United States."[20] Convinced that military action would not prevent further acts of international terrorism against the United States, Representative Barbara Lee cast the lone vote in Congress against the resolution and called for diplomatic efforts "to ensure this never happens again."[21] For holding true to her principles, Lee found herself accused of being a traitor and the subject of death threats.[22]

Janis Besler Heaphy, the publisher of the *Sacramento Bee*, was booed off the stage just minutes after she began to present a commencement speech at the California State University in Sacramento before an audience of seventeen thousand people in December 2001 concerning the government's response to the September 11 attacks. Heaphy's speech recognized "the validity and need for both retaliation and security." To the evident displeasure of her audience, however, she went on to ask, "[T]o what lengths are we willing to go to achieve them? Specifically, to what degree are we willing to compromise our civil liberties in the name of security?"[23]

While the intolerance encountered by Lee and Heaphy appears to have been spontaneous and unorganized, two organizations with close ties to the Bush administration have made calculated and methodical efforts to intimidate the administration's critics into silence. In November 2001, the American Council of Trustees and Alumni (ACTA), a conservative think tank founded by Lynne Cheney, the wife of Vice President Dick Cheney, issued a report grandly entitled *Defending Civilization: How Our Universities Are Failing America and What Can Be Done About It.*[24] The report accused university faculty of making statements "short on patriotism and long on self-flagellation" and went on to document 117 statements made on university campuses that in ACTA's view were objectionable because they "blame[d] America first."[25] The names of the professors who had made the statements were removed in a reissued version of the report, but not before they had been publicly circulated.[26]

Highlighted in ACTA's report was a quote from Hugh Gusterson, an anthropology professor at MIT, who had commented, "Imagine the real suffering and grief of people in other countries."[27] Gusterson reported being inundated with angry anonymous e-mails after the report's publication and expressed concern that the report would cause junior faculty members seeking tenure to keep their views to themselves.[28] Eric Foner, a professor of history at Columbia

University who was also quoted in the report, warned that ACTA "is trying to intimidate individuals who hold different points of view. There aren't loyalty oaths being demanded of teachers yet, but we seem to be at the beginning of a process that could get a lot worse and is already cause for considerable alarm."[29]

The ACTA report was followed in March 2002 with the publication of a full-page ad in the *New York Times* by the newly formed Americans for Victory over Terrorism (AVOT), an organization headed by several high-powered Republicans, including William Bennett, who served as secretary of education under President Ronald Reagan and drug czar under President George H. W. Bush. The ad criticized those "who are attempting to use this opportunity to promulgate their agenda of 'blame America first'" and concluded that their views "stem from either a hatred for the American ideals of freedom and equality or a misunderstanding of those ideals and their practice."[30] The AVOT ad documented a number of statements—not only by professors but by journalists, politicians, and others—that it found objectionable. The AVOT ad attacked President Jimmy Carter for criticizing President George W. Bush's use of the phrase "axis of evil" in his State of the Union address in January 2002 as "overly simplistic and counter-productive," and Bennett accused the former president of weakening the national resolve.[31]

AVOT and ACTA have every right under the First Amendment to criticize the viewpoints of others. But by insinuating that those with whom they disagree are unpatriotic and aid America's enemies, and by targeting the academy, where open discourse and the free exchange of ideas are so highly prized, they reveal that their true goal is to suppress dissent rather than engage in genuine dialogue.

2. PENALIZING SPEAKERS FOR THE REACTIONS OF THEIR LISTENERS

When the government penalizes speakers for the reactions of their listeners, it sanctions the heckler's veto. But the First Amendment protects controversial speech "unless shown likely to produce a clear and present danger of a serious substantive evil that rises far above public inconvenience, annoyance or unrest."[32] Justice William Douglas, speaking for the Supreme Court in *Terminiello v. Chicago*, explained that "a function of free speech under our system of government is to invite dispute," and that speech "may indeed best serve its high purposes when it induces a condition of unrest, creates dissatisfaction with conditions as they are, or even stirs people to anger."[33] As Justice Douglas warned, penalizing speakers for the reactions of their listeners leads to "the standardization of ideas, either by legislatures, courts, or dominant political or community groups."[34]

William Harvey was arrested for disorderly conduct by the New York City Police Department when his antiwar poster prompted onlookers to scream obscenities at him.[35] According to a police report, Harvey's poster displayed the World Trade Center towers with Osama Bin Laden's face superimposed on them.[36] A Manhattan Criminal Court judge denied Harvey's motion to dismiss the charges, citing Harvey's decision "to disseminate his message at a location near 'ground zero' at a time shortly after September 11."[37]

Professor Sami Al-Arian, a popular tenured professor at a public university, the University of South Florida, and a highly regarded leader of Tampa's Muslim community, was also penalized for the angry reactions of others. On September 26, 2001, Al-Arian appeared on the television show *The O'Reilly Factor*, based on the understanding that he would be asked to discuss issues of concern to the Arab-American community following September 11. Instead, the show's host, Bill O'Reilly, took the opportunity to insinuate that Al-Arian was a terrorist and to bring attention to a speech Al-Arian had delivered in 1988, at the height of the Palestinian Intifada, in which he had declared, "Death to Israel."[38] Al-Arian made clear that he was not anti-Semitic and that he was firmly opposed to the use of violence. In reaction to Al-Arian's television appearance, the University of South Florida received hateful phone and e-mail messages that included death threats against Al-Arian. The university, in a bizarre twist of logic, placed blame on Al-Arian for the "disruption" that had been caused by the anonymous individuals who had threatened his life—third parties who could hardly be characterized as under Al-Arian's control—and, turning its back on academic freedom, terminated his employment.[39]

If intolerance of unorthodox views continues unabated, Americans will soon become as adept in the art of self-censorship as the citizens of the world's most dictatorial regimes. When Americans are intimidated into keeping dissident views to themselves, our public discourse is constricted, the First Amendment is diminished, and democracy itself is under attack.

Nancy Chang

II. GUILT BY ASSOCIATION

The First Amendment protects not only freedom of expression but the freedom to associate with others for the purpose of collective political action.[40] As the Supreme Court has established, membership in an organization having both lawful and unlawful ends cannot serve as the basis for imposing guilt.[41] Rather, in the American system of justice, guilt must be personal, and it must be proved by a specific intent to further the organization's unlawful ends. These constitutional principles were developed as an antidote to the loyalty oaths and communist witch-hunts of the McCarthy era, and they remain essential to the functioning of a democratic society. But they have been tossed to the wayside by President Bush, who has vowed to bring to justice not only those who have engaged in terrorist activities but "anyone who espouses a philosophy that's terrorist."[42] This vow has been backed up by a number of post–September 11 measures that resurrect guilt by association by penalizing citizens and noncitizens solely for engaging in expressive activities on behalf of groups that the secretary of state deems terrorist.

The costs of political association have risen sharply since September 11, especially when civil disobedience and other forms of peaceful but confrontational protest activities are involved, for other reasons as well. The USA PATRI-OT Act creates a new federal crime of domestic terrorism; it appropriates funds for information-sharing systems between federal, state, and local law enforcement agencies; and it grants enhanced surveillance powers to the executive branch. As a result, political activists and the organizations with which they associate are more likely than ever to become the targets of government tracking, surveillance, and infiltration.

A. BARRING ASSOCIATION WITH DESIGNATED TERRORISTS

With the passage of the USA PATRIOT Act, the executive branch has the unprecedented authority to penalize those who associate with organizations the government considers terrorist. Anyone subject to the laws of the United States may be criminally punished for providing material support to any of the approximately thirty-three organizations that the secretary of state has designated as "foreign terrorist organizations" (FTO). In addition, immigrants may be deported for soliciting membership or funds for, or providing material support to: (1) a designated FTO, (2) one of the approximately thirty-nine organizations that have been designated on the secretary of state's "terrorist exclusion list" (TEL), or (3) an organization that has been deemed terrorist by the government but has not been designated.[43] The standards for qualifying as a terrorist organization are loose and can reach any revolutionary movement, even movements that have never directed, or threatened to direct, violence against the United States. As the ever-expanding "war on terrorism" snakes its way around the globe—from Afghanistan, to Iraq, to the Philippines, and to Colombia and other locales—the list of organizations designated as terrorist, and off-limits to Americans and immigrants living in the United States, will only grow.[44]

Nancy Chang

1. CRIMINALIZING THE PROVISION OF ALL MATERIAL SUPPORT TO DESIGNATED TERRORIST ORGANIZATIONS

Under the "material support statute," which was introduced in the Antiterrorism and Effective Death Penalty Act of 1996 (AEDPA) but was strengthened considerably in the USA PATRIOT Act, it is a crime punishable by a fifteen-year prison sentence, or by a life sentence if the death of any person results, to provide material support to any organization that the secretary of state has designated as an FTO.[45] This statute contravenes the First Amendment because it covers not only material support that furthers terrorist activities but material support that is intended solely to further a designated organization's lawful ends, such as a donation of humanitarian aid to refugee camps, schools, orphanages, or other social welfare programs under an FTO's control.[46]

In addition, the material support statute applies to the provision of "training" and "personnel" to an FTO and, since it was amended by the USA PATRIOT Act, the provision of "expert advice or assistance" as well.[47] Because the provision of almost all human services could be considered the provision of "training," "personnel," or "expert advice or assistance," the statute has the ironic effect of criminalizing political activities aimed at the peaceful resolution of conflict, such as writing an op-ed piece on behalf of the FTO, advocating the interests of an FTO before the U.S. Congress or the United Nations, representing an FTO at peace negotiations, providing an FTO organization with training on human rights advocacy or international law, or distributing an FTO's political literature.

A handful of criminal indictments have been brought

under the material support statute, including those now pending against John Walker Lindh, "the American Taliban," and civil rights attorney Lynne Stewart.[48] To date, however, the only case in which a court has ruled on the material support statute's constitutionality is a civil suit brought by the Humanitarian Law Project, an organization dedicated to protecting human rights, and other plaintiffs seeking a preliminary injunction striking down the statute as unconstitutional. The Ninth Circuit Court of Appeals rejected the plaintiffs' argument that the statute's ban on the provision of humanitarian assistance violates the First Amendment. The plaintiffs had relied on a line of Cold War–era cases establishing that guilt cannot be imposed based on one's association with an organization that has both lawful and unlawful ends in the absence of clear proof of an intent to further the organization's unlawful ends.[49] The Ninth Circuit narrowly read these cases to apply only to political speech, and not to the provision of money and goods for humanitarian purposes.[50] The Ninth Circuit agreed with the plaintiffs, however, that the terms "training" and "personnel" were unconstitutionally vague because they could be read as barring political advocacy that is clearly protected by the First Amendment, and it let stand a preliminary injunction that barred the government from criminally prosecuting the plaintiffs for providing training and personnel to designated foreign terrorist organizations.[51]

To complicate matters further, the statute under which organizations are designated as foreign terrorist organizations (FTO statute) is itself riddled with problems.[52] The FTO statute delegates to the secretary of state virtually unfettered discretion to designate as terrorist any foreign organization that has ever engaged in violence. The highly politicized nature of the designation process is illustrated by the administration's persistent failure to designate the Palestinian Liberation Organization, the Irish Republican Party, and the Northern Alliance—organizations that have resorted to violence but are now political powers with which the United States must contend. If the FTO statute had been on the books during the 1970s and 1980s, the African National Congress—another group that has resorted to violence—could have been designated as an FTO at the discretion of the secretary of state. Had the African National Congress been designated, the many thousands of Americans who volunteered their time to, and made charitable contributions toward, the group's struggle to end apartheid in South Africa might have found themselves staring at long prison sentences.

Under the FTO statute, only groups that are designated as foreign terrorist organizations may challenge their designations in court, and then only during a thirty-day window. Notably, criminal defendants who are charged with providing material support to a designated group are not permitted to do so under the statute.[53] To date, only a handful of designated foreign terrorist organizations have filed challenges. None has succeeded, at least in part because the scope of the judicial review provided for in the FTO statute is extremely limited and appears to allow the secretary of state to show the judge classified information that the group is not permitted to see, much less rebut.[54] In the first case brought under the FTO statute, a disheartened panel of the District of Columbia Court of Appeals sardonically observed that the

FTO statute left the judiciary little if any room to overrule an FTO designation, even one that was made improperly:

> [T]he record consists entirely of hearsay, none of it was ever subjected to adversary testing, and there was no opportunity for counter-evidence by the organizations affected. As we see it, our only function is to decide if the Secretary, on the face of things, had enough information before her to come to the conclusion that the organizations were foreign and engaged in terrorism. Her conclusion might be mistaken, but that depends on the quality of the information in the reports she received—something we have no way of judging.[55]

2. DETAINING AND DEPORTING NONCITIZENS FOR ASSOCIATING WITH ORGANIZATIONS DEEMED TERRORIST

In addition to having the power to punish criminally those who provide material support to a designated foreign terrorist organization, the government has the power to detain and deport noncitizens for their associations with any foreign or domestic organization that it considers terrorist, including organizations that were not designated when the association took place. According to the lexicon of Section 411 of the USA PATRIOT Act, immigrants are "engaged in terrorist activities" when they solicit membership or funds for, or provide material support to: (1) a foreign terrorist organization designated under the FTO statute, (2) a foreign or domestic group designated under the TEL provision of Section 411, or (3) an undesignated group that the secretary of state deems terrorist.[56]

Nancy Chang

Under Section 412 of the USA PATRIOT Act, a noncitizen may be held in detention, potentially indefinitely, and deported by the INS on the attorney general's certification that he has "reasonable grounds to believe" the noncitizen is engaged in terrorist activities. In the first six months that the act has been in effect, the INS has not detained or deported any noncitizens under Section 412.[57] However, in a geopolitical environment in which it is possible for the United States to provide military and financial support to the Taliban and, shortly thereafter, declare the Taliban its foremost enemy, noncitizens who maintain close contacts with social and political movements in their home countries could find themselves detained and deported with the next shift in world events.

B. THE RISING COSTS OF POLITICAL ACTIVISM

Since the Boston Tea Party, confrontational protest activities have played a vital role in the struggle for political and social justice in the United States. Our nation's independence from Great Britain, the abolition of slavery, suffrage for women, the passage of federal civil rights legislation, and the withdrawal of American troops from Vietnam were won not by academic debate but by vibrant mass movements that challenged the status quo with passion and verve.

1. THE CRITICAL ROLE OF CIVIL DISOBEDIENCE IN POLITICAL AND SOCIAL JUSTICE MOVEMENTS

To great persuasive effect, each of these movements made principled use of nonviolent civil disobedience—acts of moral conscience in which individuals publicly and deliberately violate a law to protest government policy. Certainly the success of the American civil rights movement in breaking the stronghold of de jure, or officially sanctioned, racial segregation is largely attributable to the courageous and inspirational examples of Rosa Parks, who was arrested in Montgomery, Alabama, for sitting in the white section of a bus and refusing to move back to the black section; Martin Luther King Jr., who was beaten and jailed for sitting down at whites-only lunch counters in defiance of the South's Jim Crow laws; Fred Shuttlesworth, who was fire-hosed and set upon by dogs for leading peaceful marches in protest of segregated schools in Birmingham, Alabama; and thousands of others who placed their lives on the line for the cause of racial equality.

Drawing inspiration from the writings of Henry David Thoreau and Mohandas K. Gandhi, Dr. King wrote from a prison cell in Birmingham that civil disobedience was integral to the struggle to win civil rights for African-Americans:

> I submit that an individual who breaks a law that conscience tells him is unjust and who willingly accepts the penalty of imprisonment in order to arouse the conscience of the community over its injustice, is in reality expressing the highest respect for law.... [T]he present tension in the South is a necessary phase of the transition from an obnoxious negative peace, in which the Negro passively accepted his unjust plight, to a substantive and positive peace, in which all men will respect the dignity and worth of human personality. Actually, we who engage in nonviolent direct action are not the creators of tension. We merely bring to the surface

the hidden tension that is already alive. We bring it out in the open, where it can be seen and dealt with. Like a boil that can never be cured so long as it is covered up but must be opened with all its ugliness to the natural medicines of air and light, injustice must be exposed, with all the tension its exposure creates, to the light of human conscience and the air of national opinion before it can be cured.[58]

2. INTELLIGENCE GATHERING ON POLITICAL ACTIVISTS IN THE POST–SEPTEMBER 11 WORLD

By violating the law through acts of civil disobedience, protesters expose themselves to rough treatment at the hands of arresting officers, lengthy imprisonment under harsh and unsafe conditions, the emotional and financial drain of defending themselves against criminal charges, the imposition of hefty fines and long prison sentences, the stigma of a criminal conviction, and the loss of earnings. Notwithstanding their inherently expressive nature, acts of civil disobedience do not receive the protection of the Constitution except when the law being violated is itself ruled unconstitutional. A law that a protester firmly believes to be unconstitutional and has deliberately violated in order to challenge it in court may be upheld, or struck down only on appellate review following years of contentious litigation.

The costs of non-violent but confrontational protest activities, already considerable before September 11, have since risen sharply. Political activists and the organizations with which they associate are more likely than ever to become the targets of government monitoring, infiltration, disruption, and criminal prosecution as the result of the USA PATRIOT Act's creation of a broad new crime of domestic terrorism; the act's appropriation of substantial additional funding toward improving the Department of Justice's Regional Information Sharing System (RISS), a secure Intranet information sharing system that is accessed by over 5,600 federal, state, and local law enforcement agencies; and increased monitoring of political activities by federal, state, and local law enforcement agencies. With Attorney General Ashcroft's issuance of permissive new guidelines on the gathering of domestic intelligence on May 30, 2002, the stage has been set for a replay of the worst abuses of the FBI's infamous COINTELPRO program.

a. Civil Disobedience as Domestic Terrorism

As discussed in chapter 1, the USA PATRIOT Act defines a new federal crime of domestic terrorism that stretches beyond recognition the common understanding of the term "terrorism" as premeditated and politically motivated violence targeted against a civilian population.[59] The new crime's wide ambit covers any "acts dangerous to human life that are a violation of the criminal laws," if they "appear to be intended...to influence the policy of a government by intimidation or coercion" and if they "occur primarily within the territorial jurisdiction of the United States."[60] The looseness of this definition allows the government to group nonviolent civil disobedience in the tradition of Thoreau, Gandhi, and King together with the Al Qaeda network's ruthless attacks on civilians, all under the single banner of terrorism. Acts of civil disobedience that take place in the

112

United States necessarily meet three of the five elements in the definition of domestic terrorism: they constitute a "violation of the criminal laws," they are "intended...to influence the policy of a government," and they "occur primarily within the territorial jurisdiction of the United States." Many acts of civil disobedience, including the blocking of streets and points of egress by nonviolent means during a demonstration or sit-in, could be construed as "acts dangerous to human life" that appear to be intended to influence the policy of a government "by intimidation or coercion," in which case they would meet the crime's two remaining elements. Spontaneous clashes between protesters and police officers in the course of a heated demonstration could also be construed as acts falling within the crime's reach.

As a result, protest activities that previously would most likely have ended in a charge of disorderly conduct under a local ordinance can now lead to federal prosecution and conviction for terrorism. Experience has taught us that when prosecutors are entrusted with the discretion to file trumped-up charges for minor crimes, politically motivated prosecutions and the exertion of undue pressure on activists who have been arrested to turn state's witness against their associates, or to serve as confidential informants for the government, are not far behind.

b. Electronic Dossiers for Internet-Age Political Activists
The broad sweep of the new crime of domestic terrorism also places political activists engaged in peaceful protest activities at risk of having their dossiers indexed in a RISS database where they can be instantaneously accessed by

thousands of federal, state, and local law enforcement offices.[61] Prior to the passage of the USA PATRIOT Act, suspected terrorists could not be indexed in RISS's databases unless they were linked to a specific violent act, and domestic terrorism was not yet a crime.[62] But as a senior RISS official, Gerald Lynch, recently confirmed, "[T]he Patriot Act will make it easier to place [individuals suspected of terrorism] in some form of database so they can be looked at very carefully."[63]

Although RISS's operations are shrouded in secrecy, its capabilities are clearly enormous. And these capabilities are certain to increase as the result of a provision in the USA PATRIOT Act that appropriates $50 million for fiscal year 2002 and $100 million for fiscal year 2003 toward the operation of RISS in order "to enhance the investigation and prosecution abilities of participating law enforcement agencies in addressing multi-jurisdictional terrorist conspiracies and activities."[64]

By allowing information about individuals suspected of the new crime of domestic terrorism to be shared with thousands of law enforcement agencies, RISS places at risk of harm political activists who engage in, associate with those who engage in, or are suspected of engaging in civil disobedience. Information concerning activists that is personally sensitive or simply irrelevant to any legitimate law enforcement purpose, as well as erroneous or outdated information, can easily find its way into an RISS database. Once posted, this information can quickly be circulated to thousands of law enforcement offices, some of which may share the information with governmental and private organizations. The potential for arrest based on false charges, invasion of one's privacy, damage to reputation, loss of employment, or other injuries resulting from the misuse of posted information is extremely high.

c. Attorney General Ashcroft's New Domestic Intelligence-Gathering Guidelines

As described in chapter 1, the first attorney general guidelines on FBI domestic and foreign intelligence gathering were issued in 1976, in response to the Church Committee's revelations of widespread FBI surveillance, infiltration, and disruption of political groups engaged in lawful protest activities. On May 30, 2002, Attorney General John Ashcroft replaced the domestic intelligence-gathering guidelines that had been issued by Attorney General Smith[65] with new guidelines that provide FBI agents with far more latitude to engage in political surveillance.[66] Ashcroft let stand the largely classified guidelines for foreign intelligence gathering in the United States.[67]

The Ashcroft guidelines authorize FBI agents to initiate a "full investigation" "when facts or circumstances reasonably indicate that a federal crime has been, is being, or will be committed."[68] The "reasonable indication" standard is substantially lower than the probable cause needed in order to make an arrest, but it does require "specific facts or circumstances indicating a past, current, or future violation [of law]."[69] In the case of a "terrorism enterprise investigation," the FBI must have a reasonable indication that "two or more persons are engaged in an enterprise for the purpose of...furthering *political or social* goals wholly or in part through activities that involve force or violence and a violation of federal criminal law," or for the purpose of engaging in terrorism, including domestic terrorism under the USA PATRIOT Act.[70] The investigation need not be authorized by FBI headquarters.[71] Instead, a special agent in charge of an FBI field office may authorize the investigation for up to a year with notice to headquarters.[72]

In the case of a group not under a terrorism enterprise investigation, "[m]ere speculation that force or violence may occur during the course of an otherwise peaceable demonstration" is an insufficient basis for initiating an investigation. But "where facts or circumstances reasonably indicate that [the] group...has engaged in or aims to engage in activities involving force or violence [or covered criminal conduct, including engaging in domestic terrorism] in a demonstration," an investigation may be initiated.[73] In addition, the group's advocacy of non-imminent violence, which the Supreme Court held in the 1969 case of *Brandenberg v. Ohio* to be speech protected by the First Amendment,[74] may be considered in deciding to initiate a terrorism enterprise investigation.[75] In particular, statements made "in relation to or in furtherance of an enterprise's *political or social* objectives that...advocate the use of force or violence, or statements...made in furtherance of an enterprise that otherwise...advocate criminal conduct" which concern "depriving individuals of any rights secured by the Constitution or laws of the United States," weigh in favor of initiating an investigation.[76]

Once a group is under investigation, the Ashcroft guidelines do nothing to prevent the FBI from collecting information about the group's public demonstrations or its other

Nancy Chang

First Amendment–protected activities. In fact, the guidelines specifically allow the FBI to collect information on the group's members, finances, geographical dimensions, and "past and future activities and goals."[77]

When the FBI lacks the reasonable indication of criminal activities required to initiate an investigation, but "there is information or an allegation which indicates the possibility of criminal activity and whose responsible handling requires some further scrutiny beyond checking initial leads," the Ashcroft guidelines authorize FBI agents to initiate a "preliminary inquiry."[78] Preliminary inquiries may be authorized for 180 days by an FBI supervisor.[79]

Once a terrorism enterprise investigation has been initiated, the FBI may use "any lawful investigative technique," subject to compliance with Department of Justice requirements. The techniques may include the use of confidential informants, undercover activities and operations, electronic surveillance, and searches and seizures.[80] In the case of a preliminary inquiry, the FBI may use all of the techniques allowed in an investigation except for the opening of mail and nonconsensual electronic surveillance.[81] No prior authorization from a supervisory agent is required in a preliminary inquiry for the examination of records available to the public; federal, state, and local government records; interviews of the complainants, previously established informants, potential subject, and those who should readily be able to corroborate or deny the truth of the allegation; and physical and photographic surveillance.[82] The Ashcroft guidelines state, on the one hand, that "[i]nquiries and investigations shall be conducted with as little intrusion as the needs of the situation permit."[83] On the other hand, they state that "[t]he FBI shall not hesitate to use any lawful techniques consistent with these Guidelines, even if intrusive, where the intrusiveness is warranted in light of the seriousness of a crime or the strength of the information indicating its commission or potential future commission."[84]

The Ashcroft guidelines also authorize the FBI to conduct a "prompt and extremely limited checking out of initial leads" when the level of suspicion of criminal conduct is too low to support the initiation of either a full investigation or a preliminary inquiry, but the government has information of "a nature that some follow-up as to the possibility of criminal activity is warranted," Because this standard is extraordinarily vague and at best only remotely connected to suspicion of criminal conduct, it is hard to imagine any political activities that are in the least bit confrontational that would not fall within its broad sweep.

Even in the absence of any leads, the FBI "must proactively draw on available sources of information to identify terrorist threats and activities."[85] Specifically, the FBI may draw on non-profit and commercial data mining services, many of which segregate data on individuals according to their race, ethnicity, religion, citizenship status, and other characteristics; consider "information voluntarily provided by private entities" without regard to whether it was legally obtained; "visit any place and attend any event that is open to the public, on the same terms and conditions as members of the public generally"; and conduct online searches to visit webites, electronic bulletin boards, and chat rooms.[86]

Unfortunately, the Ashcroft guidelines, with their broad grant of intelligence gathering powers to the FBI, coupled with the USA PATRIOT Act's broad definition of domestic terrorism, are likely to lead to intrusive intelligence gathering on those who engage in non-violent civil disobedience or in lawful but confrontational political activities, as well as those who attract the attention of the FBI as it trolls through private databases, attends churches and mosques, and surfs the Web. With the advent of electronic record-keeping, the FBI is likely to maintain far more dossiers on law-abiding individuals and to disseminate the dossiers far more widely than during the COINTELPRO era.

d. Law Enforcement Monitoring of Political Activists

Since September 11, local police departments, with massive infusions of support and technical assistance from the Department of Justice and the FBI, have been busily refurbishing their "red squads"—the police units that became notorious during Hoover's reign as the FBI's director for spying on, infiltrating, and disrupting left-wing political organizations in cooperation with the FBI.[87] Their methods of political intelligence are varied and include reading the literature of "subversive" political groups, interviewing people who attend their rallies, infiltrating the groups, and developing informants within the groups.[88] The superintendent of the Maryland State Police, Colonel David Mitchell, revealed a few days before a recent peaceful protest against the International Monetary Fund in Washington, D.C., "I'll have troops down there.... We know there's a history of groups that are hell-bent on violence, and we've got some intelligence activity going on there too. We're keeping our ear to the ground."[89]

Even in the politically progressive city of Denver, Colorado, the police department has maintained, at least since 1999, "Spy Files" on the peaceful political activities of approximately 3,200 individuals and approximately 208 groups. Among the groups believed to have been under police surveillance are the Denver chapters of two national organizations, the American Friends Service Committee (AFSC) and Amnesty International, and local groups that focus on a range of issues, including police accountability, Native American rights, and indigenous rights in Chiapas, Mexico.[90]

In March 2002, the American Civil Liberties Union of Colorado filed a class action suit on behalf of the AFSC and several other Spy File targets, seeking an injunction ordering the Denver Police Department to halt its activities.[91] The complaint alleges that the department employed undercover operatives to videotape and photograph individuals who have participated in lawful demonstrations in the absence of a legitimate law enforcement purpose, and that the department shared information from its Spy Files with other law enforcement agencies without ensuring that these agencies would guard against the further disclosure of the information.[92] In addition, the complaint alleges that the department falsely labeled as "criminal extremist" the AFSC, a pacifist Quaker group and a recipient of the Nobel Peace Prize, and Sister Antonia Anthony, a seventy-three-year old Franciscan nun, along with other law-abiding individuals and groups. The plaintiffs charge that these practices have interfered with their ability to attract supporters to their meetings and rallies because people are fearful of having their political activities and associations monitored and recorded by the police and are concerned about being listed as associates or members of groups labeled, even falsely, as "criminal extremist."[93] The plaintiffs have charged the department with violations of the First and Fourth Amendments to the U.S. Constitution and their counterpart provisions in the Colorado State Constitution. In May 2002, the Denver Police Department filed a motion to dismiss the suit, arguing that the plaintiffs lack standing to sue.[94]

In 1972, the Supreme Court slammed the door to the courthouse on a similar set of plaintiffs—anti–Vietnam War protesters who claimed that their exercise of their First Amendment rights had been chilled by extensive army surveillance of, and data gathering on, their public meetings and protest activities.[95] In *Laird v. Tatum*, the Court held that plaintiffs who challenge government surveillance of their public activities must show a "specific present objective harm or a threat of specific future harm," and not simply a "subjective chill" on their political expression, in order to have standing to sue.[96] The *Tatum* Court recognized that when government regulations, such as loyalty oaths, chill speech, they are unconstitutional even though they "fall short of a direct prohibition against the exercise of First Amendment rights."[97] However, the Court refused to extend the reach of the First Amendment to situations in which "the chilling effect arise[s] merely from the individual's knowledge that a governmental agency was engaged in certain activities or from the individual's concomitant fear that, armed with the fruits of those activities, the agency might in the future take some other and additional action detrimental to that individual."[98] The Court concluded that the plaintiffs had presented "[a]llegations of a subjective 'chill'" that were "not an adequate substitute for [the] claim of specific present objective harm or a threat of specific future harm" required for standing to sue.[99]

Some, though not enough, inroads have been made into the Supreme Court's holding in *Tatum*. When political activists have alleged that government intelligence-gathering activities have been conducted in the absence of a legitimate law enforcement purpose, for a politically motivated purpose, by illicit means, or in ways that are likely to cause injury beyond a "subjective chill," courts have distinguished *Tatum* and found standing to sue. In one such case, the Third Circuit Court of Appeals followed *Tatum* only to the extent of holding that a group of political activists did not have standing to sue the Philadelphia Police Department for photographing them and gathering information on them at public meetings. But the Third Circuit Court of Appeals allowed the activists to press their suit against the department for dispersing information collected on their political activities to governmental agencies and private organizations for non-law-enforcement purposes and for disclosing the information on nationwide television.[100] The Third Circuit questioned how such a dispersal of information "could be considered within the proper ambit of law enforcement activity, particularly since it is alleged that the plaintiffs are subject to surveillance only because their political views deviate from those of the 'establishment.'"[101] In addition, the Third Circuit expressed concern that such a dispersal of information could interfere with the job opportunities, careers or travel rights of the individual plaintiffs and such practical consequences may ensue without any specific awareness on plaintiffs' part. The mere anticipation of the practical consequences of joining or remaining with plaintiff organizations may well dissuade some individuals from becoming members, or may persuade others to resign their membership.[102]

Whether the Denver Police Department's surveillance of political activists and groups engaged in peaceful protest activities represents the norm or an aberration among federal, state, and local police departments is a matter about which we can only speculate at this time. However, if the AFSC plaintiffs defeat the department's motion to dismiss their complaint, we may learn a great deal about how police conduct political intelligence operations.

What chance would the civil rights movement have stood of bringing about an end to de jure racial segregation in the 1950s and 1960s if it had been operating under today's rules of surveillance? Rosa Parks, Martin Luther King Jr., Fred Shuttlesworth, and the activists who stood beside them could have been charged with the crime of domestic terrorism for their acts of nonviolent civil disobedience. Their every move, their political activities, their personal relationships, their financial transactions, and their private records could have been monitored and recorded. And their dossiers could have been indexed in a law enforcement database and shared instantaneously with local police departments throughout the Deep South. The freedom to express dissenting viewpoints and to associate with others who share them without fear of government interference or retaliation is the hallmark of a vibrant and healthy democracy. But the changes wrought in the USA PATRIOT Act and Attorney General Ashcroft's guidelines on domestic intelligence gathering are poised to stifle dissent. One wonders what these changes portend for today's movements for political and social justice and for our democracy as a whole.

III. THE RISE OF GOVERNMENT SECRECY

The events of September 11 have been used as a pretext not only for expanding the powers of the executive branch but also for restricting the ability of the public, the press, and even Congress to gain access to the information necessary in order to hold the executive accountable for its actions. As discussed in chapter 3, the Bush administration has aggressively fought off requests made under the Freedom of Information Act and a New Jersey State Right to Know Law seeking information concerning the two thousand or so individuals who have been placed in detention in the course of the government's investigation of September 11, and it has sought to close the immigration proceedings of detainees of special interest through its issuance of Chief Immigration Judge Michael Creppy's directive to all immigration judges and an accompanying interim rule. The Bush administration has reduced public access to government records, persuaded the press to narrow its coverage of the military response to the September 11 attacks, admitted that it planned to circulate disinformation to the foreign press, and rebuffed requests from Congress for information on executive actions. By keeping the public, the press, and Congress in the dark, the executive has prevented meaningful participation in government decision making and oversight, and it has thereby undermined the democratic principles that underlie the First Amendment and our system of separation of powers.

A. RESTRICTIONS ON GOVERNMENT RECORDS

In October 1993, President Bill Clinton issued a memorandum to federal agency heads in which he encouraged public access to government records through the Freedom of Information Act:

> For more than a quarter century now, the Freedom of Information Act has played a unique role in strengthening our democratic form of government. The statute was based upon the fundamental principle that an informed citizenry is essential to the democratic process and that the more the American people know about their government the better they will be governed. Openness in government is essential to accountability and the Act has become an integral part of that process.[103]

In an accompanying memorandum, Attorney General Janet Reno urged the "maximum responsible disclosure of information" in response to FOIA requests, explaining that "the American public's understanding of the workings of its government is a cornerstone of our democracy."[104]

But the policy of openness in government operations that characterized the Clinton administration has been replaced by a policy of secrecy. In a memorandum to agency heads dated October 12, 2001, Attorney General Ashcroft strongly discouraged the disclosure of information under FOIA:

> Any discretionary decision by your agency to disclose information protected under the FOIA should be made only after full and deliberate consideration of the institutional, commercial and personal privacy interests that could be implicated by disclosure of the information..... When you carefully consider FOIA requests and decide to withhold records, in whole or in part, you can be assured that the Department of Justice will defend your decisions unless they lack a sound legal basis or present an unwarranted risk of adverse impact on the ability of other agencies to protect other important records.[105]

Larry Klayman, the executive director of Judicial Watch, an organization that has close to one hundred pending FOIA actions, has described the Bush administration's attitude toward requests for information as one of "arrogance throughout—that the government is not to be questioned."[106] Certainly the Department of Justice has been parsimonious in its response to FOIA requests filed in October 2001 by civil rights groups seeking the identities of individuals detained in connection with the government's post–September 11 antiterrorism investigation.[107]

In addition, President Bush has taken measures to restrict access to President Reagan's records, which were scheduled for release under the Presidential Records Act of 1978 on January 20, 2001.[108] President Bush delayed the release of these records for months on end, and on November 1, 2001, he issued an executive order that essentially overrides the act by executive fiat.[109] Faced with the Watergate scandal and President Nixon's assertion of proprietary claims over the records and tape recordings created during his administration, Congress passed the act in order to ensure public ownership and control over presidential records. Under the act, a president's records are to be opened for inspection twelve years after he leaves office. But President Bush's executive order grants the incumbent president, as well as former presidents, vice presidents, and their representatives, the power to veto the release of records based on a simple claim of executive privilege. With the executive order, historian Stanley Kutler warns, "[T]he shadowy doctrine of executive privilege has been elevated to a personal right, extending a lifetime and even beyond."[110] In Kutler's words:

Let's be perfectly clear: Bush's action has nothing whatsoever to do with protecting the nation. It has everything to do with protecting our exclusive club of ex- and future ex-presidents. Most immediately, he is also covering for Reagan's vice president, as his [executive] order, incredibly, extends executive privilege to that office as well. Who knows? Perhaps we might learn something about that vice president's role in Iran-Contra, a role for which he famously denied any knowledge.[111]

In February 2002, the American Historical Association, Stanley Kutler, and other organizations and individuals with an interest in the historical records of former presidents and vice presidents filed suit against the National Archives and Records Administration.[112] The suit charges that the executive order is in direct violation of the express will of Congress in the Presidential Records Act and therefore falls outside of President Bush's constitutional authority, which is limited to the faithful execution of the laws. The suit seeks an order requiring the national archivist to release presidential papers without regard to the executive order.

At the same time that the Bush administration has restricted the release of information under FOIA and the Presidential Records Act, it has quietly removed information from the public domain.[113] On March 19, 2002, White House Chief of Staff Andrew Card sent a memorandum to agency heads calling for "an immediate reexamination of current measures for identifying and safeguarding…information that could be misused to harm the security of our Nation and the safety of the people."[114] A companion memorandum from Laura Kimberly of the Department of Justice's Information Security Oversight Office called upon agency heads to protect carefully against the "inappropriate disclosure" of "sensitive" information that has not been classified.[115] According to OMB Watch, which has been maintaining a list of materials that have been removed from government Web sites since

September 11, thirteen federal agencies have "depublished" information.[116] Although the publication of information concerning weapons of mass destruction poses a genuine threat to our security, the term "sensitive" is so vague that it could encompass information that the government simply finds embarrassing or annoying.[117]

B. A COMPLIANT PRESS CENSORS ITSELF

Historically, the press has played a crucial watchdog role over government operations. In 1971, the Supreme Court refused to block the *New York Times* and the *Washington Post* from publishing, over the strong objections of the Nixon administration, a classified study of the Vietnam War that exposed the government's use of secrecy and deception to gain the public's support for the war. The study, which has come to be known as the Pentagon Papers, had been commissioned by President Johnson's secretary of state, Robert McNamara, and was leaked to the press, in an act of civil disobedience, by Daniel Ellsberg. As Justices Hugo Black and William Douglas explained in their concurring opinion:

> In the First Amendment the Founding Fathers gave the free press the protection it must have to fulfill its essential role in our democracy.... The press was protected [from government censorship] so that it could bare the secrets of government and inform the people. Only a free and unrestrained press can effectively expose deception in government. And paramount among the responsibilities of a free press is the duty to prevent any part of the govern-

ment from deceiving the people and sending them off to distant lands to die of foreign fevers and foreign shot and shell.[118]

The Bush administration's strict supervision over the release of information concerning its military campaign has prevented the press from "bar[ing] the secrets of government and inform[ing] the people."[119] And the press, for its part, has shown itself far too willing to comply with White House requests that it limit its news coverage. On October 10, 2001, the five major television news organizations—ABC News, CBS News, NBC News, the Cable News Network, and Fox News Channel—announced that they had reached a joint agreement to abridge future videotaped statements from Osama bin Laden and his followers. The organizations were persuaded to enter into this unprecedented pact by National Security Advisor Condoleeza Rice, who had offered her unsubstantiated speculation that the videos could contain coded messages. But as pointed out by a network executive who chose to remain anonymous, "What sense would it make to keep the tapes off the air if the message could be found transcripted in newspapers or on the Web? The videos could also appear on the Internet. They'd get the message anyway."[120]

Emboldened by Rice's success with the television news organizations, the next day, October 11, 2001, White House Press Secretary Ari Fleischer announced that he would ask newspapers to enter into an agreement similar to that reached by the television news organizations.[121] The response of Howell Raines, the editor of the *New York*

Times, was equivocal. While Raines stated that "our practice is to keep our readers fully informed," he also added that "[w]e are always available to listen to any information about security issues."[122]

Even more troubling than the timidity of the television news organizations are signs that the press has been censoring itself. At least two newspaper columnists were fired for criticizing President Bush's actions on September 11. Dan Guthrie, an award-winning columnist for the *Grants Pass Daily Courier* in Oregon, wrote a column entitled "When the Going Gets Tough, the Tender Turn Tail," in which he accused President Bush of "hiding in a Nebraska hole" on September 11, in an act of "cowardice."[123] A week later, the paper's publisher fired Guthrie, and the editor ran a front-page apology for having printed Guthrie's column. In a similar scenario, Tom Gutting of the *Texas City Sun* was fired for writing a column in which he accused President Bush of "flying around the country like a scared child" on September 11, and the paper's publisher ran a front-page apology for having printed Gutting's column.[124] These attacks on journalistic freedom send a clear message to all members of the press that they would be wise to fall in line behind White House Press Secretary Ari Fleischer and "watch what they say."

C. GOVERNMENT-ISSUED DISINFORMATION

The Bush administration's efforts to control the news go far beyond its requests to television and newspaper organizations to refrain from releasing the full statements of Osama bin Laden and his followers. On February 19, 2002, the *New*

York Times reported that the Pentagon's newly created Office of Strategic Influence was planning to disseminate false information to foreign journalists, produce propaganda, and carry out "black ops," including sabotage and attacks against foreign information systems.[125] With its secret exposed, Secretary of Defense Donald Rumsfeld announced that the Office of Strategic Influence would be closed.[126] Despite Secretary Rumsfeld's announcement, speculation continues that the Office of Strategic Influence's operations have been taken over by other offices.[127] And, as columnist Art Buchwald was quick to note, Rumsfeld's announcement was not inconsistent with the possibility that he "was putting out the denial at the request of the Office of Strategic Influence."[128]

D. REFUSING TO ANSWER TO CONGRESS

With the expansion of executive powers since September 11, the need for congressional oversight to guard against the abuse of these powers is all the more acute. Yet, by its repeated failures to cooperate with Congress's requests for information, the Bush administration has placed our constitutional system of checks and balances in danger.

Citing an alleged leak of classified information, an angry President Bush informed his cabinet by memorandum dated October 5, 2001, that "until you receive further notice from me," only eight members of Congress—the House Speaker and minority leader, Senate majority and minority leaders and the chairmen and ranking minority members on the intelligence committees—would be briefed on classified and sensitive national security matters.[129] Before the president backed down from this threat to cut off the flow of information to Congress, Senator John Kerry of Massachusetts, one of the members of the intelligence committees who would have been shut out by this limitation, complained, "We just cannot do our job as U.S. senators without updated briefings and relevant information."[130]

The standoff between the Senate and Homeland Security Director Tom Ridge in the spring of 2002 suggests that Congress may lack the ability to play an effective oversight role in the face of stiff resistance from the Bush administration. On March 4, 2002, Senator Robert Byrd, chair of the Senate Appropriations Committee, wrote a letter to Ridge asking him to testify before the Committee. Included in the Senate's growing list of concerns are the scope of Ridge's authority; how the Bush administration's $38 billion budget request for domestic security programs would be spent; why the INS issued visa extensions on March 11, 2002, to Mohamed Atta and Marwan al-Shehhi (two of the suicide hijackers involved in the September 11 attacks); and why the administration failed to inform Congress of its plans for a contingency government in case of catastrophic attack.[131] The Administration refused to allow Ridge to testify before the committee, citing his status as a presidential advisor rather than a cabinet member.[132] This refusal prompted Senator Tom Daschle to threaten to subpoena Ridge in order to obtain his testimony by compulsion,[133] and it prompted Senator Richard Shelby to dub Ridge "the homeland security czar."[134] Senator Kerry, who pledged that he and others in Congress would continue to raise questions about the war's direction, remarked, "Those who try to stifle the vibrancy of our democracy and shield policy from scrutiny [under] the false cloak of patriotism miss the real value of what our troops defend and how we best defend our troops."[135]

The political freedoms guaranteed to us by the First Amendment—the freedom of speech and association, the right to assemble and to petition the government for redress of grievances, and the freedom of the press—are essential to our stability as a nation. As Justice Brandeis observed:

> Those who won our independence...knew that it...is hazardous to discourage thought, hope and imagination; that fear breeds repression; that repression breeds hate; that hate menaces stable government; that the path of safety lies in the opportunity to discuss freely supposed grievances and proposed remedies; and that the fitting remedy for evil counsels is good ones.[136]

But the Bush administration has chosen to disregard these wise words. Invoking the crisis at hand, the administration has warned Americans to watch what they say, imposed guilt by association, and prevented the public, the press, and Congress from overseeing their actions. These measures are designed to silence political dissent, and they threaten the vitality of our democracy.

CHAPTER 5

RECLAIMING OUR CIVIL LIBERTIES

The antiterrorism measures discussed in this book have placed our civil liberties in jeopardy. And because the "war on terrorism"—of which these measures form a part—is likely to become a permanent feature of American life, the task of reclaiming our civil liberties in the post–September 11 world will not be an easy one. We must exercise our constitutionally protected rights of free speech and political association to protest antiterrorism measures that infringe on political and personal freedoms, organize public education campaigns, engage in grassroots organizing, build broad coalitions, reach out to people of faith and immigrant communities, participate in voter education and registration drives, alert the mainstream and alternative press to our concerns, write letters to the editor for publication in our local newspapers, and seek information from the government under the Freedom of Information Act. In addition, we must call upon the judiciary to serve as a check against executive and legislative measures that violate the Constitution. And we must call upon Congress to play an oversight role over the executive branch, pass corrective legislation where needed, and appoint judges who are sensitive to the Bill of Rights.

Our efforts must be directed not only at the federal level but at state and local governments as well. Since September 11, more than a thousand antiterrorism measures have been proposed in state and local jurisdictions across the nation, and already a number of them have become law.[1] These measures threaten to criminalize speech and protest activities, limit the availability of public records, expand government surveillance powers, and promote participation in acts the legislature deems patriotic.[2]

Unfortunately, noncitizens who engage in political activities today run the risk of being placed in detention and deported under the USA PATRIOT Act or for minor immigration violations. Noncitizens from Arab and South Asian countries are being selectively targeted by the Department of Justice for "voluntary interviews," and in campaigns to deport "absconders." It is critical that citizens engage in political activities on their behalf.

The decision whether this nation will uphold the Bill of Rights—or acquiesce in its surrender—will ultimately fall to the judiciary. In the nine months since September 11, four trial court judges have issued rulings finding antiterrorism measures to be illegal, in defiance of a tradition in which the judiciary has bowed to the wishes of the political branches of government in times of crisis.[3] Justice William Brennan, in a 1987 speech presented in Jerusalem, urged that we "build bulwarks of liberty that can endure the fears and frenzy of sudden danger—bulwarks to help guarantee that a nation fighting for its survival does not sacrifice those national values that make the fight worthwhile."[4] There is wisdom in his words. Our best hope for the peaceful resolution of conflict and our future safety lies in the expansion, rather than the contraction, of the democratic values set forth in the Constitution.

NOTES

INTRODUCTION

1.   Statement of U.S. Senator Russell Feingold, "On the Anti-Terrorism Bill," 25 October 2001, available at http://www.senate.gov/~feingold/releases/01/10/102501at.html.

2.   Judith Miller and Don Van Natta Jr., "In Years of Plots and Clues, Scope of Qaeda Eluded U.S.," *New York Times*, 9 June 2002.

CHAPTER 1

1.   James Madison, *The Federalist*, no. 47, ed. Isaac Krammick (1987), 304.

2.   The first three articles of the U.S. Constitution enumerate the powers of the three branches of our federal government. Congress's powers are set forth in Article I; the powers of the executive branch are set forth in Article II; and the judiciary's powers are set forth in Article III.

3.   *Myers v. United States*, 272 U.S. 52, 85 (1926) (J. Brandeis, dissenting).

4.   The First Amendment to the U.S. Constitution provides that "Congress shall make no law respecting an establishment of religion, or prohibiting the free exercise thereof; or abridging the freedom of speech, or of the press; or the right of the people peaceably to assemble, and to petition the Government for a redress of grievances."

5.   See *New York Times Co. v. Sullivan*, 376 U.S. 254, 270 (1964).

6.   The Fourth Amendment to the U.S. Constitution provides that "the right of the people to be secure in their persons, houses, papers, and effects, against unreasonable searches and seizures, shall not be violated, and no warrants shall issue, but upon probable cause, supported by oath or affirmation, and particularly describing the place to be searched, and the persons or things to be seized."

7.   The probable cause requirement of the Fourth Amendment requires that law enforcement officers have reasonably trustworthy knowledge of facts and circumstances that are sufficient to warrant a prudent person to believe that an offense has been or is being committed. See, e.g., *Brinegar v. United States*, 338 U.S. 160, 175-76 (1949). This requirement is not met by a mere hunch or guess.

v. United States, 338 U.S. 160, 175-76 (1949). This requirement is not met by a mere hunch or guess.

8. The due process clause of the Fifth Amendment to the U.S. Constitution provides that "no person shall...be deprived of life, liberty, or property, without due process of law."

9. See *United States v. Salerno,* 481 U.S. 739, 746 (1987).

10. See *Mathews v. Eldridge,* 424 U.S. 319 (1976).

11. The equal protection clause of the Fourteenth Amendment to the U.S. Constitution provides that "no State shall...deny to any person within its jurisdiction the equal protection of the laws." The equal protection clause applies to the state and local governments through the Fourteenth Amendment and to the federal government through the Fifth Amendment.

12. The Sixth Amendment to the U.S. Constitution provides that "in all criminal prosecutions, the accused shall enjoy the right to a speedy and public trial, by an impartial jury...and to be informed of the nature and cause of the accusation; to be confronted with the witnesses against him; to have compulsory process for obtaining witnesses in his favor, and to have the assistance of counsel for his defence."

13. The suspension clause is found in Article I, Section 9, Clause 2, of the U.S. Constitution and provides that "the privilege of the writ of habeas corpus shall not be suspended, unless when in cases of rebellion or invasion the public safety may require it."

14. Specifically, the act defined a new crime of seditious libel as the "writ[ing], print[ing], utter[ing] or publish[ing of]...any false, scandalous, and malicious writing" with the intent of bringing the U.S. government or its officials into "contempt or disrepute." See 5th Cong., 74, 1 Stat. 596 (1798) (expired 1801).

15. Leonard Weintraub, "Crime of the Century: Use of The Mail Fraud Statute Against Authors," *Boston University Law Review* 67 (May 1987): 507, 519.

16. 65th Cong. 75, 40 Stat. 553 (1918).

17. *Schenck v. United States,* 249 U.S. 47, 51 (1919).

18. *Schenck v. United States,* 52.

19. Howard Zinn, *A People's History of the United States: 1942 to Present* (1999) 366.

20. *Debs v. United States*, 249 U.S. 211, 214 (1919).

21. Zinn, *A People's History*, 368.

22. 76th Cong., 439, 54 Stat. 671 (1940).

23. *Dennis v. United States*, 341 U.S. 494 (1951).

24. Ibid., 510.

25. Ibid.

26. *Yates v. United States*, 354 U.S. 298 (1957).

27. *Brandenberg v. Ohio*, 395 U.S. 444, 447–48 (1969).

28. Ibid., 446.

29. See, e.g., *Dennis v. United States*, 341 U.S. 494 (1951).

30. Victor Navasky, *Naming Names* (1980).

31. See, e.g., *Joint Anti-Fascist Refugee Committee v. McGrath*, 341 U.S. 123 (1951); *Konigsberg v. State Bar of California*, 366 U.S. 36 (1961); *American Communications Ass'n v. Douds*, 339 U.S. 382 (1950).

32. *Communist Party of the United States v. Subversive Activities Control Board*, 367 U.S. 1 (1961).

33. Alan Bigel, "The First Amendment and National Security: The Court Responds to Governmental Harassment of Alleged Communist Sympathizers," *Ohio Northern University L. Rev.* 19 (1993): 883, 890.

34. *Barenblatt v. United States*, 360 U.S. 109 (1959).

35. Ibid.,126.

36. See *Wilkinson v. United States*, 365 U.S. 399 (1961); *Braden v. United States*, 365 U.S. 431 (1961), reh'g denied, 365 U.S. 890 (1961). See also Frank Wilkinson, "Revisiting the 'McCarthy Era': Looking at *Wilkinson v. United States* in Light of *Wilkinson v. Federal Bureau of Investigation*," *Loyola of Los Angeles L. Rev.* 33 (January 2000): 681.

37. See *American Communications Ass'n v. Douds*, 382.

38. See *Communist Party of the United States v. Subversive Activities Control Board*, 1.

39. *Scales v. United States*, 367 U.S. 203, 229 (1961), reh'g denied, 367 U.S. 978 (1961).

40. *United States v. Robel*, 389 U.S. 258, 262 (1967).

41. See, e.g., *NAACP v. Claiborne Hardware Co.*, 458 U.S. 886, 932 (1982); *Healy v. James*, 408 U.S. 169 (1972).

42. *United States v. Robel*, 264.

43. Ward Churchill and Jim Vander Wall, *The COINTELPRO Papers: Documents from the FBI's Secret Wars against Dissent in the United States*, 177 (1990).

44. See Senate Select Committee to Study Governmental Operations with Respect to Intelligence Activities, *Intelligence Activities and the Rights of Americans*, Final Report, Book II, 94th Cong., 2d sess., 1976, S. Rept. 94-755, 67.

45. Ibid., 67.

46. Ibid., 11.

47. Ibid.

48. Ibid., 87.

49. Ibid., 89.

50. Ibid., 10, 68.

51. Ibid., 15.

52. Frank Donner, *The Age of Surveillance: The Aims And Methods of America's Political Intelligence System* (1980), 195–203.

53. *National Intelligence Reorganization and Reform Act of 1978*, 95th Cong., S. 2525.

54. *United States Attorney General Guidelines on Domestic Security Investigation* (1976).

55. *United States Attorney General Guidelines on General Crimes, Racketeering Enterprise and Domestic Security/Terrorism Investigations* (1989) (Smith guidelines), available at http://www.usdoj.gov/ag/ readingroom/generalcrimea.htm.

56. *The Attorney General's Guidelines on General Crimes, Racketeering Enterprise and Terrorism Enterprise Investigations* (2002) (Ashcroft guidelines), available at http://www.usdoj.gov/olp/generalcrimes2.pdf. See also Adam Liptak, "Changing the Standard: Despite Civil Liberties Fears, F.B.I. Faces No Legal Obstacles on Domestic Spying," *New York Times*, 31 May 2002, A1.

57. Smith guidelines at Part III.B.

58. Ibid. at Part II.C.

59. Ibid. at Part I.

60. Ibid. at Part IV.B.3.

61. Kenneth J. Cooper, "Clinton Tempers Anti-Terrorist Bill; Power to Bar Fund-Raising for Designated Groups is Dropped," *Washington Post*, May 4, 1995, p. A28; Stephen Labaton, "Terror in Oklahoma Security; U.S. is Easing Restrictions on Monitoring Some Groups," *New York Times*, 3 May 1995, B14.

62. Smith guidelines at Part II.B.

63. Ibid.

64. Ibid. at Part II.B(6).

65. *United States Attorney General Guidelines for FBI Foreign Intelligence Collection and Foreign Counterintelligence Investigations* (1995), available at http://www.usdoj.gov/agreadingroom/terrorisminte12.pdf; Senate Select Committee on Intelligence, the FBI and CISPES, 101st Congress, 1st Session 91 (1989).

66. "Law Professors' Petition to Congress to Enact Legislation that Will Prevent the FBI and Other Law Enforcement Agencies from Undertaking Investigations that Threaten the Exercise of the First Amendment," reproduced in James Dempsey and David Cole, *Terrorism and the Constitution*, Appendix (2002).

67. Don Edwards, "Reordering the Priorities of the FBI in Light of the End of the Cold War," *St. John's L. Rev.* (1991): 59, 72. Representative Don Edwards, a former FBI agent, served as the chair of the Civil and Constitutional Rights Subcommittee of the House Judiciary Committee and was a champion of the First Amendment. Edwards played a critical role in the congressional inquiry into the FBI's CISPES investigation.

68. Ibid.

69. James Dempsey and David Cole, *Terrorism and the Constitution*(2002), 22–24.

70. See Abby Scher, "The Crackdown on Dissent," *The Nation*, 5 February 2001, 23.

71. *Ex Parte Merryman*, Fed. Cas. 9487 (C.C. Md. 1861).

72. *Ex Parte Milligan*, 71 U.S. 2 (1866).

73. Ibid., 120–21.

74. See Edwin P. Hoyt, *The Palmer Raids 1919–20: An Attempt to Suppress Dissent* (1969).

75. Executive Order No. 9066, 7 F.R. 1402, 19 February 1942.

76. See Eric Yamamoto et al., *Race, Rights, and Reparation: Law and the Japanese Internment* (2001).

77. See Philip Tajitsu Nash, *Moving for Redress, Yale L.J.* 94(1994): 743.

78. *Korematsu v. United States*, 323 U.S. 214, 223 (1944).

79. Ibid.

80. Ibid., 242 (J. Murphy, dissenting).

81. *Korematsu v. United States*, 584 F. Supp. 1406 (N.D.Ca. 1984). The Latin term "coram nobis" literally means "error before us." A writ of coram nobis is brought by an individual who has been criminally convicted, not to reargue points of law that have been decided but to raise errors of fact, including the prosecutor's knowing withholding of facts from the individual and the judge. The petitioner must demonstrate that there was a fundamental error or manifest injustice in the decision—an exceedingly high burden of proof.

82. Ibid., 1413.

83. See *Civil Liberties Act of 1988*, 50 U.S.C. §§ 1989 et seq.

84. Ibid.

85. See, e.g., *Wygant v. Jackson Bd. of Educ.*, 476 U.S. 267, 280 n.6 (1984).

86. See *Korematsu v. United States*, 323 U.S. 236 (J. Murphy, dissenting); see also *Stenberg v. Carhart*, 530 U.S. 914, 953 (2000) (J. Scalia, dissenting).

CHAPTER 2

1. The USA PATRIOT Act is, "with a label like that, hard to criticize in any way." William Safire, "Acronymania: Creating Weird Titles to Spell Catchy Words," *New York Times Magazine*, 24 February 2002, 13. The full title of the USA PATRIOT Act is the Uniting and Strengthening America by Providing Appropriate Tools Required to Intercept and Obstruct Terrorism Act of 2001, Pub. L. No. 107–56.

2. Adam Clymer, "Antiterrorism Bill Passes; U.S. Gets Expanded Powers," *New York Times*, 26 October 2001, A1; Robin Toner and Neil A. Lewis, "House Passes Terrorism Bill Much Like Senate's, but With 5-Year

Limit," *New York Times*, 13 October 2001, B6; Jonathan Krim, "Anti-Terror Push Stirs Fears for Liberties; Rights Groups Unite To Seek Safeguards," *Washington Post*, 18 September 2001, A17; Mary Leonard, "Civil Liberties," *Boston Globe*, 21 September 2001, A13.

3. Adam Clymer, "Bush Quickly Signs Measure Aiding Antiterrorism Effort," *New York Times*, 27 October 2001, B5.

4. This book uses the term "noncitizen" in lieu of the interchangeable term "alien." Both of these terms broadly encompass not only "immigrants"— a group that includes legal permanent residents, refugees, and asylees— but also "nonimmigrants," including visa holders who have been admitted on a temporary basis, such as tourists and students, and temporary workers. These terms also include individuals whose immigration status in the United States is undocumented.

    In addition, this book uses the term "deportation" in lieu of the term "removal," which was introduced to the Immigration and Nationality Act in 1996, to refer to any governmental removal of a person from the United States under the immigration laws.

5. *USA PATRIOT Act* § 802, amending 18 U.S.C. § 2331(5).

6. The silencing effect that the new crime of domestic terrorism is likely to have on political dissent in this country is discussed in detail in chapter 4.

7. *USA PATRIOT Act* § 411(a), amending 8 U.S.C. §1182(a)(3)(B)(i)(IV)(bb).

8. *USA PATRIOT Act* § 411(a), amending 8 U.S.C. §1182(a)(3)(B)(i)(VI).

9. See 8 U.S.C. §§ 1182(a)(27) and (28) (1982).

10. See *Kleindienst v. Mandel*, 408 U.S. 753 (1972).

11. *Kyllo v. United States*, 533 U.S. 27, 40 (2001).

12. Ibid.

13. See *USA PATRIOT Act* § 224(a).

14. See *USA PATRIOT Act* § 224(b).

15. Ted Bridis, "Number of U.S. Wiretaps Down Last Year," Associated Press, 30 April 2002.

16. Ibid.

17. Miles Bensor, "Tech Firms Feel Heat as U.S. Snoops on Citizens," *Times Picayune*, 28 April 2002, 1.

18. Ibid.

19. Ibid.

20. Ibid.

21. Ibid.

22. Ibid.

23. Ibid.

24. Robyn Blumner, "Book Police Thwarted by Colorado Ruling," *Milwaukee Journal Sentinel,* 16 April 2002, 13A.

25. See *USA PATRIOT Act* § 208, amending 50 U.S.C. § 1803(a); Neil Lewis, "After Sept. 11, a Little-Known Court Has a Greater Role," *New York Times,* 3 May 2002, A20.

26. *USA PATRIOT Act* § 213, amending 18 U.S.C. § 3103a. The definition of the term "adverse result" in Section 213 is borrowed from a statute establishing the standards under which the government may provide delayed notice when it searches stored e-mail and other wire and electronic communications—searches that are not nearly as intrusive as physical searches of one's home or office. The term is defined in 18 U.S.C. § 2705(a)(2) as: "(A) endangering the life or physical safety of an individual; (B) flight from prosecution; (C) destruction of or tampering with evidence; (D) intimidation of potential witnesses; or (E) otherwise seriously jeopardizing an investigation or unduly delaying a trial."

27. *Wilson v. Arkansas,* 514 U.S. 927, 929 (1995).

28. 899 F.2d 1324, 1337 (2d Cir. 1990).

29. 800 F.2d 1451, 1456 (9th Cir. 1986).

30. See http://www.cdt.org/security/011030doj.

31. *USA PATRIOT Act* § 215, amending 50 U.S.C. §§ 1862 and 1863.

32. 50 U.S.C. § 1801 et seq.

33. *USA PATRIOT Act* § 215, amending 50 U.S.C. 1862(a)(1).

34. *USA PATRIOT Act* § 215, amending 50 U.S.C. § 1862(c)(1).

35. See 18 U.S.C. § 1862(b)(2)(B), prior to its amendment by *USA PATRIOT Act* § 215.

36. FISA defines the term "United States persons" to include United States citizens and lawful permanent residents. See 50 U.S.C. § 1801(i).

37. *USA PATRIOT Act* § 215, amending 50 U.S.C. § 1862(a)(1).

38. See U.S.C. § 1862(a), prior to its amendment by *USA PATRIOT Act* § 215.

39. *USA PATRIOT Act* § 215, amending 50 U.S.C. § 1862.

40. *USA PATRIOT Act* § 215, amending 50 U.S.C. § 1863.

41. Pen registers record telephone numbers of outgoing calls. See 18 U.S.C. § 3127(3). Trap and trace devices record telephone numbers from which incoming calls originate. See 18 U.S.C. § 3127(4).

42. *USA PATRIOT Act* § 216(c)(3) amending 18 U.S.C. § 3127(4) (emphasis added).

43. *USA PATRIOT Act* § 216(b) amending 18 U.S.C. § 3123(a).

44. In the case of orders for pen registers and trap and trace devices, the Electronic Communications Privacy Act of 1986 demands only "a certification by the applicant that the information likely to be obtained is relevant to an ongoing criminal investigation." 18 U.S.C. §§ 3122(b)(2). See also *Smith v. Maryland*, 442 U.S. 735 (1979). However, providing telephone dialing information does not reveal the contents of telephone communications.

45. *USA PATRIOT Act* §216 (b) amending 18 U.S.C. § 3123(a)(3)(A).

46. *Internet and Data Interception Capabilities Developed by the FBI*, Statement of Dr. Donald M. Kerr, Assistant Director, Laboratory Division, 24 July 2000.

47. *USA PATRIOT Act* § 216(b) amending 18 U.S.C. § 3123(b)(3).

48. Undated Letter of Assistant Attorney General Daniel Bryant, 9 (emphasis added). This letter was sent to Senators Bob Graham, Orrin Hatch, Patrick Leahy, and Richard Shelby while the USA PATRIOT Act was under consideration by Congress. A copy of the letter is on file with the author.

49. 50 U.S.C. §§ 1804(a)(7)(B) and 1823(a)(7)(B) (emphasis added).

50. *USA PATRIOT Act* § 218, amending 50 U.S.C. §§ 1804(a)(7)(B) and 1823(a)(7)(B) (emphasis added).

51. *United States v. United States District Court for the Eastern District of Michigan*, 407 U.S. 297 (1972).

52. Ibid., 313.

53. Ibid., 320.

54. Ibid.

55. Ibid., 317.

56. Ibid., 309 (emphasis added).

57. 50 U.S.C. § 1801(a)(5).

58. *United States v. Truong Dinh Hung*, 629 F.2d 908, 915 (4th Cir. 1980) (emphasis added).

59. *United States v. Johnson*, 952 F.2d 565, 572 (9th Cir. 1992).

60. The exclusionary rule is a judicially created rule that bars prosecutors from using incriminating evidence obtained in violation of the Fourth Amendment to prove guilt. See, e.g., *Mapp v. Ohio*, 367 U.S. 643, 655 (1961).

61. *USA PATRIOT Act* § 203(a), (b), and (d). The information that may be shared must "involve" either "foreign intelligence or counterintelligence," as that term is defined in the National Security Act of 1947, at 50 U.S.C. § 401a, or "foreign intelligence information," as that term is defined in Section 203(a)(1), (b)(2)(C), and (d)(2).

62. *USA PATRIOT Act* § 203(a), amending Rule 6(e)(3)(C) of the Federal Rules of Criminal Procedure.

63. See *In re Schofield*, 486 F.2d 85, 90 (3d Cir. 1973); *United States v. Calandra*, 414 U.S. 338, 343 (1974) (allowing the grand jury's consideration of suppressed evidence).

64. *In re Schofield*, 486 F.2d at 90.

65. See, e.g., *United States v. Dionisio*, 410 U.S. 1 (1973).

66. Section 1001 of Title 18 of the *U.S. Code* provides in relevant part that "whoever, in any matter within the jurisdiction of the executive, legislative, or judicial branch of the Government of the United States, knowingly and willfully—(1) falsifies, conceals, or covers up by any trick, scheme, or device a material fact; (2) makes any materially false, fictitious, or fraudulent statement or representation; or (3) makes or uses any false writing or document knowing the same to contain any materially false, fictitious, or fraudulent statement or entry; shall be fined under this title or imprisoned not more than 5 years, or both." See 18 U.S.C. § 1001(a).

67. See, e.g., *United States v. Calandra*, 414 U.S. 338, 343 (1974).

68. See Keeney and Walsh, *The American Bar Association's Grand Jury Principles: A Critique From a Federal Criminal Justice Perspective, Idaho L. Rev.* 14 (1978): 545.

69. See Rule 6(e) of the Federal Rules of Criminal Procedure. See also *United States v. Procter & Gamble Co.*, 356 U.S. 677, 681 (1958). The grand jury secrecy rules also serve "(1) to prevent the escape of those whose indictment may be contemplated; (2) to insure the utmost freedom to the grand jury in its deliberations, and to prevent persons subject to indictment or their friends from importuning the grand jurors; (3) to prevent subornation of perjury or tampering with the witnesses who may testify before grand jury and later appear at the trial of those indicted by it;…and (5) to protect the innocent accused who is exonerated from disclosure of the fact that he has been under investigation, and from the expense of standing trail where there was no probability of guilt." Ibid.

70. *USA PATRIOT Act* § 203(b), amending 18 U.S.C. § 2517(6).

71. *USA PATRIOT Act* §§ 203(d) and 905(a).

72. Select Committee to Study Governmental Operations with Respect to Intelligence Activities, *Intelligence Activities and the Rights of Americans, Final Report of the Senate Select Committee to Study Governmental Operations with Respect to Intelligence Activities*, 94th Cong., 2d sess., 1976.

73. Under the INA, which is codified at 8 U.S.C. §§ 1100 et seq., noncitizens who have or are engaged in "terrorist activities" or activities that threaten the national security are subject to deportation from the United States. See 8 U.S.C. § 1227(a)(4)(A) and (B).

74. Since 1983, the U.S. government has defined the term "terrorism," "for statistical and analytical purposes," as the "premeditated, politically motivated violence perpetrated against noncombatant targets by subnational groups or clandestine agents, usually intended to influence an audience." See preface and introduction of *Patterns of Global Terrorism 2001*, U.S. Department of State (May 2002), xvi, available at http://www.state.govdocuments/organization/10286.pdf.

75. *USA PATRIOT Act* § 411(a), amending 8 U.S.C. §1182(a)(3)(B)(iii)(V)(b).

76. *USA PATRIOT Act* § 411(a), amending 8 U.S.C. §1182(a)(3)(B)(iv)(IV)(bb) and (cc), (V)(bb) and (cc), and (VI)(cc) and (dd).

77. The Supreme Court has described guilt by association as "alien to the traditions of a free society and the First Amendment itself." *NAACP v. Claiborne Hardware Co.*, 458 U.S. 886, 932 (1982). *See also Healy v. James*, 408 U.S. 169, 186 (1972).

78. *USA PATRIOT Act* § 411(a) amended 8 U.S.C. §1182(a)(3)(B)(vi)(I) to include as a "terrorist organization" any foreign organization so designated by the secretary of state under 8 U.S.C. § 1189, a provision that was introduced in the Antiterrorism and Effective Death Penalty Act of 1996. As of March 27, 2002, the secretary of state had designated thirty-three organizations as foreign terrorist organizations under 8 U.S.C. § 1189. These designations appear in the Fed. Reg. at 67 Fed. Reg. 14761 (27 March 2002); 66 Fed. Reg. 66492 (26 December 2001); 66 Fed. Reg. 51088-90 (5 October 2001); 66 Fed. Reg. 47054 (10 September 2001); and 66 Fed. Reg. 27442 (16 May2001). In order to qualify as a designated "foreign terrorist organization" under 8 U.S.C. §1182(a)(3)(B)(vi)(I), the secretary of state must find that "(A) the organization is a foreign organization; (B) the organization engages in terrorist activity; and (C) the terrorist activity of the organization threatens the security of United States nationals or the national security of the United States." See 8 U.S.C. § 1189(a)(1)(A)-(C).

In addition, USA PATRIOT Act § 411(a) amended 8 U.S.C. §1182(a)(3)(B)(vi)(II) to include as a "terrorist organization" any domestic or foreign organization so designated by the Secretary of State in consultation with or upon the request of the attorney general under Section 411. On December 5, 2001, the secretary of state, in consultation with the attorney general, designated thirty-nine groups as Terrorist Exclusion List organizations under Section 411(a)(1)(G) of the USA PATRIOT Act. See 66 Fed. Reg. 63620 (7 December 2001). In order to qualify as a designated "terrorist organization" under this provision, a "finding" must be made that the organization engages in one or more of the following "terrorist activities": (1) "commit[ting] or incit[ing] to commit, under circumstances indicating an intention to cause death or serious bodily injury, a terrorist activity;" (2) "prepar[ing] or plan[ning] a terrorist activity;" and (3) "gather[ing] information on potential targets for terrorist activity." See 8 U.S.C. § 1182(a)(3)(B)(iv)(I)-(III).

79. *USA PATRIOT Act* § 411(a), amending 8 U.S.C. §1182(a)(3)(B)(vi)(III). In order to qualify as an undesignated "terrorist organization" under 8 U.S.C. §1182(a)(3)(B)(vi)(III), "a group of two or more individuals, whether organized or not," must engage in one or more of the "terrorist activities" described in 8 U.S.C. § 1182(a)(3)(B)(iv)(I)-(III).

80. *USA PATRIOT Act* § 411(a), amending 8 U.S.C. § 1182(a)(3)(B)(iv)(IV)(cc), (V)(cc), and (VI)(dd).

81. *USA PATRIOT Act* § 411(c)(3)(A) and (B).

82. *USA PATRIOT Act* § 412(a), adding 8 U.S.C. § 1226A(a).

83. *USA PATRIOT Act* § 412(a), adding 8 U.S.C. § 1226A(a)(3) and (5).

84. See, e.g., *Terry v. Ohio*, 392 U.S. 1, 20–22 (1968).

85. *USA PATRIOT Act* § 412(a), adding 8 U.S.C. § 1226A(a)(2).

86. *USA PATRIOT Act* § 412(a), adding 8 U.S.C. § 1226A(a)(7).

87. *USA PATRIOT Act* § 412(a), adding 8 U.S.C. § 1226A(b)(1) and (2)(A)(iii) and (iv).

88. The INS's regular practice is to release nonimmigrants on bond except in situations where the noncitizen poses either a threat to security or a risk of flight on bond. See *Reno v. Flores*, 507 U.S. 292, 294-95 (1993); *Matter of Patel*, 15 I. & N. 666 (1976). Under Section 412, a noncitizen's dangerousness is presumed based on the one-sided certification of the attorney general, and the noncitizen is not provided with an opportunity to rebut the certification.

89. While the USA PATRIOT Act does not explicitly authorize the use of secret evidence in immigration proceedings, Sections 411 and 412 are likely to encourage its use. The INS has long taken the position that it is authorized to use secret evidence in bond proceedings. See, e.g., *Al Najjar v. Reno*, 97 F.Supp.2d 1329 (S.D.Fl. 2000); *Kiareldeen v. Reno*,71 F.Supp.2d 402 (D.N.J. 1999). The author is one of the attorneys representing the plaintiffs in these two cases.

90. See *INS v. Lopez-Mendoza*, 468 U.S. 1032 (1984); *Fong Haw Tan v. Phelan*, 33 U.S. 6, 10 (1948).

91. *USA PATRIOT Act* § 412(a), adding 8 U.S.C. § 1226A(a)(2).

92. *USA PATRIOT Act* § 412(a), adding 8 U.S.C. § 1226A(a)(6).

93. *USA PATRIOT Act* § 412(a), adding 8 U.S.C. § 1226A(b)(1).

CHAPTER 3

1. Not discussed in this chapter are three highly controversial executive orders that President Bush has issued since September 11. First, Executive Order 13224 blocks the property of, and prohibits transactions with, "persons designated by the executive branch as having committed, threatened to commit, or supported terrorism." See 66 Fed. Reg. 49079 (24 September 2001). Second, Executive Order 13233 imposes restrictions on public access to presidential papers. See 66 Fed. Reg. 56025 (1 November 2001).

This executive order and a lawsuit charging that it violates the Presidential Records Act of 1978 are discussed in chapter 4. Third, Executive Order 57833 establishes, in the absence of legislative authorization, a military tribunal that will have the ability to try in secret noncitizens suspected of terrorism. See 66 Fed. Reg. 57831 (13 November 2001).

The Supreme Court has delineated the power of the executive to engage in lawmaking in the absence of congressional authorization. In *Youngstown Sheet & Tube Co. v. Sawyer*, 343 U.S. 579 (1952), the Court struck down an executive order issued by President Harry Truman that would have allowed the government to seize and operate steel factories during the Korean War in order to prevent a nationwide strike of steel workers. The Court explained that "in the framework of our Constitution, the President's power to see that the laws are faithfully executed refutes the idea that he is to be a lawmaker. The Constitution limits his functions in the lawmaking process to the recommending of laws he thinks wise and the vetoing of laws he thinks bad." Ibid., 587.

2. See 5 U.S.C. § 553.

3. See, e.g., Mark Fineman, "A Case of Where, Not What; Prosecutors Say Zacarias Moussaoui's Travels–from an Afghan Terrorist Training Camp to an Oklahoma Flight School–Are Key to His Indictment in the Sept. 11 Attacks," *Los Angeles Times*, 30 March, 2002, A1.

4. Attorney General John Ashcroft, Press Briefing, 18 September 2001, available at http://www.usdoj.gov/ag/agcrisisremarks9_18.htm.

5. See David Firestone and Christopher Drew, "Al Queda Link Seen in Only a Handful of 1,200 Detainees, *New York Times*, 29 November 2001, A1; Todd S. Purdum, "Ashcroft's About-Face on the Detainees," *New York Times*, 28 November 2001, B7; Amy Goldstein and Dan Eggen, "U.S. to Stop Issuing Detention Tallies," *Washington Post*, 9 November 2001.

6. David Cole, "Enemy Aliens," *Stanford L. Rev.* 54 (2002): 951, 958.

7. See 5 U.S.C. § 552.

8. See Amnesty International, *Amnesty International's Concerns Regarding Post September 11 Detentions in the USA* (14 March 2002), 8–9, available at http://web.amnesty.org/ai.nsf/Index/AMR510442002?OpenDocument &of=COUNTRIES\USA.

9. Jim Edwards, "Stay on Release of Detainee Names Leads to Chaos for Sept. 11 Cases," *New Jersey Law Journal* 168 (29 April 2002): 337.

10. Jeffrey Gold, "Judge Bars Blanket Closure of Detainee Deportation Hearings," Associated Press, 30 May 2002.

11. See *Zadvydas v. Davis*, 533 U.S. 678 (2001); *Matter of Patel*, 15 I & N Dec. 666, 667 (BIA 1976).

12. *United States v. Awadallah*, 2002 WL 755793, *2 (S.D.N.Y. 30 April 2002).

13. See 18 U.S.C. § 3144. Approximately twenty-six individuals detained on material witness warrants have been publicly identified. See Plaintiffs' Reply in Support of Their Cross-Motion for Summary Judgment and Opposition to Defendant's Motion for Summary Judgment in *Center for National Security Studies, et al., v. Department of Justice*, Civil Action No. 01-2500 (D. D.C.), 16, available at http://www.cnss.gwu.edu/ ~cnss/cnssreplyinsupprt.htm.

14. See Christopher Drew and Judith Miller, "Though Not Linked to Terrorism, Many Detainees Cannot Go Home," *New York Times*, 18 February 2002; David Firestone & Christopher Drew, "Al Qaeda Link Seen In Only a Handful of 1,200 Detainees, *New York Times*, 29 November 2001, A1; Richard A. Serrano, "Rights Ensnarled in Dragnet; Immigration Statutes Used to Hold Suspects Indefinitely and Detain Material Witnesses," *Seattle Times*, 27 September 2001, A6.

15. Tamar Lewin, "The Domestic Roundup: As Authorities Keep Up Immigration Arrests, Detainees Ask Why They Are Targets," *New York Times*, 31 January 2002.

16. Ibid.

17. Ibid.

18. Susan Sachs, "U.S. Defends the Withholding of Jailed Immigrants' Names," *New York Times*, 21 May 2002, A17.

19. Section 412 of the USA PATRIOT Act is described in detail in chapter 2.

20. Tom Brune, "U.S. Evades Curbs in Terror Law," *Newsday*, 26 April 2002, A17.

21. Ibid.

22. See 66 Fed. Reg. 48334 (20 September 2001) (amending 8 C.F.R. § 287.3(d)).

23. *Zadvydas v. Davis*, 533 U.S. 678 (2001).

24. *USA PATRIOT Act* § 412(a), adding 8 U.S.C. § 1226A(a)(3) and (5).

25. *Center for National Security Studies, et al., v. Department of Justice*, Civ. No.01-2500 (D. D.C.).

26. Amnesty International Report at 11. See also Dan Eggen, "Long Wait for Filing Charges Common for Sept. 11 Detainees," *Washington Post*, 19 January 2002, A12; Jim Edwards, "Data Show Shoddy Due Process for Post–Sept. 11 Immigration Detainees," *New Jersey Law Journal* 167 (6 February 2002): 361.

27. Amnesty International Report, 11.

28. Ibid.

29. Attorney General John Ashcroft, "Prepared Remarks for the U.S. Mayors Conference," 25 October 2001, available at http://www.usdoj.gov/ag/speeches/2001/agcrisisremarks10_25.htm. See also Dan Eggen, "Tough Anti-Terror Campaign Pledged," *Washington Post*, 26 October 2001, A1; Karen Gullo, "Ashcroft Discusses New Powers," Associated Press, 25 October 2001.

30. Tamar Lewin, "The Domestic Roundup."

31. See 66 Fed. Reg. 54909 (31 October 2001) (amending 8 C.F.R. § 3.19(i)(2)).

32. Jim Edwards, "Attorneys Face Hidden Hurdles in September 11 Detainee Cases," *New Jersey Law Journal* 166 (3 December 2001): 789.

33. Christopher Drew and Judith Miller, "Though Not Linked to Terrorism."

34. Ibid.

35. See *Turkmen, et al., v. Ashcroft, et al.*, CV 02-2307 (E.D.N.Y.). A copy of the complaint in this action is available at http://news.findlaw.com/hdocs/docs/terrorism/turkmenash41702cmp.pdf. The author is one of the attorneys representing the plaintiffs in this suit.

36. See *County of Riverside v. McLaughlin*, 500 U.S. 44 (1991).

37. See *United States v. Awadallah*, 2002 WL 755793 (S.D.N.Y. 30 April 2002).

38. Ibid., *23.

39. Wayne Washington, "More Opposition to Detentions in Terror Probe," *Boston Globe*, 13 May 2002, A1.

40. Richard A. Serrano, "Isolation, Secrecy Veil Most Jailed in Roundup Investigation," *Los Angeles Times*, 4 November 2001, A1; "A Deliberate Strategy of Disruption; Massive, Secretive Detention Effort Aimed

Mainly at Preventing More Terror," *Washington Post*, 4 November 2001, A1; Jim Edwards, "Attorneys Face Hidden Hurdles"; Andrew Gumbel, "The Disappeared," *Independent*, 26 February 2002, p.1.

41. Ibid.

42. Robyn Blumner, "INS Transfer Procedures Making a Mockery of Detainee Rights," *St. Petersburg Times*, 4 January 2002.

43. Amnesty International Report, 21.

44. Ibid., 19–20.

45. Ibid., 16.

46. Ann Davis, "Why Detainees So Often Waive Right to Counsel," *Wall Street Journal*, 8 February 2002, B1.

47. Ibid.

48. The lawsuit, *Center for National Security Studies, et al., v. Department of Justice*, Civ. No.01-2500 (D. D.C.), was brought by the American Civil Liberties Union, the American Immigration Law Foundation, the American Immigration Lawyers Association, Amnesty International USA, the Arab American Institute, the American-Arab Anti-Discrimination Committee, the Asian American Legal Defense and Education Fund, the Center for Constitutional Rights, the Center for Democracy and Technology, the Center for National Security Studies, the Council on American Islamic Relations, the Electronic Privacy Information Center, the First Amendment Foundation, Human Rights Watch, The Multiracial Activist, The Nation Magazine, the National Association of Criminal Defense Lawyers, the National Black Police Association, the Partnership for Civil Justice, People for the American Way Foundation, the Reporters Committee for Freedom of the Press, and the World Organization Against Torture, USA. Copies of the key documents in this lawsuit are available at http://www.gwu.edu/~cnss/.

49. See Affidavit of James Reynolds, Chief of the Terrorism and Violent Crimes Section of the Department of Justice's Criminal Division, Civ. No.01-2500 (D. D.C. 2002), available at http://www.cnss.gwu.edu/~cnss/dojreynoldsdeclaration.htm; Affidavit of Dale Watson, Civ. No.01-2500 (D. D.C. 2002), available at http://www.cnss.gwu.edu/~cnss/watsonaffidavit.pdf.

50. Ibid.

51. Plaintiffs' Reply in Support of Their Cross-Motion for Summary Judgment and Opposition to Defendant's Motion for Summary Judgment in *Center for National Security Studies, et al., v. Department of Justice*, Civil Action No. 01-2500 (D. D.C.).

52. Ibid., 11.

53. Ibid., 12–13.

54. Ibid.

55. *American Civil Liberties Union, et al., v. County of Hudson, et al.*, No. HUD-L-463-02 (N.J. Superior Ct., 2002).

56. Siobahn Roth, "Yellow Flag for DOJ: Several Judges Have Taken Shots at Anti-terror Tactics; Will Others Follow?" *Legal Times*, 28 May 2002; Seth Stern, "Courts Roll Back Secrecy in War on Terror," *Christian Science Monitor*, 15 May 2002, 4; CBS, "Judge: Let ACLU See Names," CBSNEWS.com, 27 March 2002, available at http://www.cbsnews.com/stories/2002/03/27/national/main504735.shtml. See also http://www.judiciary.state.nj.us/ditalia/aclu.htm.

57. Susan Sachs, "U.S. Defends the Withholding of Jailed Immigrants' Names," *New York Times*, 21 May 2002, A7.

58. "Release of Information Regarding Immigration and Naturalization Service, Detainees in Non-Federal Facilities," 67 Fed. Reg. 19508 (22 April 2002) (to be codified at 8 C.F.R. §§ 236 and 241).

59. William Glaberson, "Closed Immigration Hearings Criticized as Prejudicial," *New York Times*, 7 December 2001. A copy of the Creppy directive is available at http://news.findlaw.com/hdocs/docs/aclu/creppy092101memo.pdf.

60. See *Detroit Free Press v. Ashcroft*, 195 F.Supp.2d 937, 943 (E.D. Mich. 2002).

61. 8 C.F.R. §§ 3.27 and 240.10. See also *Pechter v. Lyons*, 441 F. Supp. 115 (S.D.N.Y. 1977).

62. See, e.g., *Richmond Newspapers, Inc. v. Virginia*, 448 U.S. 555 (1980); *Brown & Williamson Tobacco Corp. v. FTC*, 710 F.2d 1165 (6th Cir. 1983); *Fitzgerald v. Hampton*, 467 F.2d 755 (D.C. Cir. 1972).

63. Steve Fainaru, "U.S. Loses a Ruling on Secret Detention," *Washington Post*, 30 May 2002, A01.

64. *North Jersey Media Group v. Ashcroft*, No. 02-967 (D. N.J. 30 May 2002), at 37. The author is one of the attorneys representing the media plaintiffs in this suit.

65. Ibid., 30–31.

66. Ibid., 31.

67. Ibid.

68. Ibid.

69. *Detroit Free Press v. Ashcroft*, 195 F.Supp.2d 937, 944 (E.D. Mich. 2002). Rabih Haddad has filed a companion suit to the *Detroit Free Press* suit that challenges the Creppy directive on due process grounds, *Haddad v. Ashcroft*, No. 02-70605 (E.D. Mich.). Haddad's suit is currently pending before Judge Edmunds. The author is one of the attorneys representing Rabih Haddad in this suit.

70. *Detroit Free Press v. Ashcroft*, No. 02-1437 (6th Cir., 18 April 2002).

71. "Protective Orders in Immigration Administrative Proceedings," 67 Fed. Reg. 36799 (28 May 2002).

72. Amnesty International Report, 28–32.

73. Ibid., 33–34.

74. Ibid., 33.

75. Complaint in *Turkmen v. Ashcroft*, paragraphs 85–88.

76. Amnesty International Report, 34.

77. Seve Fainaru, "Jordanian Detainee Testifies on Abuse; Student Alleges Kicks and Threats," *Washington Post*, 15 February 2002.

78. Ibid.

79. Ibid., 29–30.

80. Ibid., 39.

81. Somini Sengupta, "Ill-Fated Path to America, Jail and Death," *New York Times*, 5 November 2001.

82. Ibid.

83. Ibid.

84. Siobahn Roth, "Yellow Flag for DOJ."

85.   "Special Administrative Measure for the Prevention of Acts of Violence and Terrorism," 66 Fed. Reg. 55062 (31 October 2001) (amending 28 C.F.R. §501.3(d)).

86.   Ibid.

87.   Ibid.

88.   Ibid.

89.   Ibid.

90.   *Upjohn Co. v. United States*, 449 U.S. 383, 389 (1981).

91.   See *Zolin v. United States*, 491 U.S. 554, 572 (1989); *United States v. De La Jara*, 973 F.2d 746, 748 (9th Cir. 1992).

92.   See *Strickland v. Washington*, 466 U.S. 668 (1984); *Gideon v. Wainwright*, 372 U.S. 335 (1965).

93.   *Weatherford v. Bursey*, 429 U.S. 545 (1977); *United States v. Johnson-El*, 878 F.2d 1043 (8th Cir. 1989).

94.   *Al'Owhali v.Ashcroft*, 02 Cv. 00883 (D. D.C.).

95.   Deborah Rhode, "Terrorists and Their Lawyers," *New York Times*, 16 April 2002, A27; Dennis Duggan, "Unpopular Job Now Dangerous," *Newsday*, 10 April 2002, A2.

96.   The federal indictment against Lynne Stewart is available at http://news.findlaw.com/hdocs/docs/terrorism/ussattar040902ind.pdf.

97.   Mark Hamblett, "Defense Bar Mobilizes Behind Stewart," *New York Law Journal*, 28 May 2002; Lisa Anderson and Cam Simpson, "U.S. Lawyer Indicted in Terror Case," *Chicago Tribune*, 10 April 2002, 1.

CHAPTER 4

1.   *West Virginia State Board of Education v. Barnette*, 319 U.S. 624, 642 (1943).

2.   Harvey A. Silverglate, "First Casualty of War," *National Law Journal*, 3 December 2002, A21.

3.   See Richard Huff, "White House Sees Red Over Maher's Remarks," *Daily News* (New York), 27 September 2001, 112.

4.   *Anti-Terrorism Policy Review: Before the Senate Committee on the Judiciary*, 6 December 2001, 2001 WL 26188084 (statement of John Ashcroft, Attorney General).

5. See Matthew Rothschild, "Ashcroft: My Critics Are Traitors!" *The Progressive*, 8 December 2001. Article III, Section 3, of the U.S. Constitution provides "Treason against the United States, shall consist only in levying War against them, or in adhering to their enemies, giving them Aid and Comfort."

6. Kris Axtman, "Political Dissent Can Bring Federal Agents to Door," *Christian Science Monitor*, 8 January 2002; Emil Guillermo, "The FBI's House Calls," *SF Gate*, 18 December 2001, available at http://www.sfgate.com/cgi-bin/article.cgi?file=/gate/archive/2001/12/18/eguillermo.DTL.

7. Ibid.

8. Matthew Rothschild, "The New McCarthyism," *The Progressive*, January 2002, 18.

9. Ibid.

10. Ibid.

11. *Watts v. United States*, 394 U.S. 705, 704 (1969).

12. Ibid., 706. See also 18 U.S.C. § 871(a).

13. *Rankin v. McPherson*, 483 U.S. 378 (1987).

14. Ibid., 381.

15. Ibid.

16. See *United for a Stronger America: Citizens' Preparedness Guide*, available at http://www.ojp.usdoj.gov/ojpcorp/cpg.pdf.

17. Dan Eggen, "Neighborhood Watch Enlisted in Terror War; Citizens Urged to Step Up in $2 Million Expansion," *Washington Post*, 7 March 2002, A1.

18. Bill Berkowitz, "AmeriSnitch," *The Progressive*, May 2002, 27.

19. Ibid., 28.

20. "Authorization for Use of Military Force," Pub. L.No. 107-40 § 2, 115 Stat. 224 (14 September 2001).

21. Marc Cooper, "Rep. Barbara Lee: Rowing Against the Tide," *Los Angeles Times*, 23 September 2001, 4M; Daniel Borenstein, "Anti-War Vote by California Congresswoman Gets Attention," *Contra Costa Times*, 21 September 2001.

22. Marianne Constantinou, "Barbara Lee; Rep. Lee, Committed to Ideals, Takes Heat for Vote against Bush," *San Francisco Chronicle*, 26

September 2001, A1; Todd J. Shriber, "Lee Put Under Guard in Washington After 'No' Vote," *Bloomberg News*, 19 September 2001; " 'No'-Vote Pol Under Guard," *New York Post*, 18 September 2001, 28.

23. Timothy Egan, "In Sacramento, a Publisher's Questions Draw the Wrath of the Crowd," *New York Times*, 19 December 2001, B1; Robert Salladay, "Fallout Continues from Interrupted Sacramento Speech," *San Francisco Chronicle*, 19 December 2001, 14.

24. American Council of Trustees and Alumni, "Defending Civilization: How Our Universities Are Failing America and What Can Be Done About It," (November 2001), 3, available at http://www.goacta.org/ Reports/def-civ.pdf.

25. Ibid.

26. Eric Scigliano, "Naming–and Un-naming–Names," *The Nation*, 31 December 2001.

27. Ibid., 2.

28. Tom Mashberg. "Pro or Con, War Talk's Risky on Campus," *Boston Herald*, 16 December 2001.

29. Matthew Rothschild, "The New McCarthyism," 23.

30. David Corn, "Soundbyte Patriots," *Alternet*, 15 March 2002, available at http://www.alternet.org/print.html?StoryID=12612; Jim Lobe, "The War on Dissent Widens," *Alternet*, 12 March 2002, available at http://www.alternet.org/print.html?StoryID=12637.

31. Ibid.

32. *Terminiello v. Chicago*, 337 U.S. 1, 4 (1949).

33. Ibid.

34. Ibid., 5.

35. Nat Hentoff, "Judge Ross vs. Free Speech," *Village Voice*, 28 February 2002, 31; Tom Perotta, "Man Faces Trial for Public Stir over bin Laden," *New York Law Journal*, 1 February 2002, 1 (citing *People v. Harvey*, 2001-NY-078439 (New York Cty. Crim. Ct.).

36. Ibid.

37. Ibid.

38. "Protecting Speech on Campus," *New York Times*, 27 January 2002, Sec. 4, 12.

39. Ibid.

40. See, e.g., *NAACP v. Alabama ex rel. Patterson*, 357 U.S. 449 (1958); *Bates v. City of Little Rock*, 361 U.S. 516 (1960).

41. See *United States v. Robel*, 389 U.S. 258, 262 (1967); *Scales v. United States*, 367 U.S. 203, 229 (1961), reh'g denied, 367 U.S. 978 (1961). See also *NAACP v. Claiborne Hardware Co.*, 458 U.S. 886, 932 (1982).

42. David E. Sanger, "Bush, on Offense, Says He Will Fight to Keep Tax Cuts," *New York Times*, 6 January 2002, A1.

43. As of March 27, 2002, the secretary of state had designated thirty-three organizations as foreign terrorist organizations under 8 U.S.C. § 1189. See These designations appear in the Fed. Reg. at 67 Fed. Reg. 14761 (27 March 2002); 66 Fed. Reg. 66492 (26 December 2001); 66 Fed. Reg. 51088-90 (5 October 2001); 66 Fed. Reg. 47054 (10 September 2001); and 66 Fed. Reg. 27442 (16 Mary 2001). In order to qualify as a designated "foreign terrorist organization" under 8 U.S.C. §1182(a)(3)(B)(vi)(I), the secretary of state must find that "(A) the organization is a foreign organization; (B) the organization engages in terrorist activity; and (C) the terrorist activity of the organization threatens the security of United States nationals or the national security of the United States." See 8 U.S.C. § 1189(a)(1)(A)-(C).

   On December 5, 2001, the secretary of state, in consultation with the attorney general, designated thirty-nine groups as Terrorist Exclusion List organizations under Section 411(a)(1)(G) of the USA PATRIOT Act. See 66 Fed. Reg. 63620 (7 December 2001). In order to qualify as a designated "terrorist organization" under this provision, a "finding" must be made that the organization engages in one or more of the following "terrorist activities": (1) "commit[ting] or incit[ing] to commit, under circumstances indicating an intention to cause death or serious bodily injury, a terrorist activity;" (2) "prepar[ing] or plan[ning] a terrorist activity;" and (3) "gather[ing] information on potential targets for terrorist activity." See 8 U.S.C. § 1182(a)(3)(B)(iv)(I)–(III).

44. See Robert Dreyfuss, "Colin Powell's List," *The Nation*, 25 March 2002.

45. Section 2339B(a) of Title 18 of the *U.S. Code*, as amended by USA PATRIOT Act § 810(c) and (d), provides in relevant part, "Whoever, within the United States or subject to the jurisdiction of the United States, knowingly provides material support or resources to a foreign terrorist organization, or attempts or conspires to do so, shall be fined under this title or imprisoned not more than 15 years, or both, and if the death of any person results, shall be imprisoned for any term of years or for life."

46. The term "material support or resources" for the purposes of 18 U.S.C. § 2339B(a) is defined as "currency or monetary instruments or financial securities, financial services, lodging, training, expert advice or assistance, safehouses, false documentation or identification, communications equipment, facilities, weapons, lethal substances, explosives, personnel, transportation, and other physical assets, except medicine or religious materials." See 18 U.S.C. § 2339A(b), as amended by USA PATRIOT Act § 805(a)(2).

47. See *USA PATRIOT Act* § 805(a)(2)(B), amending 18 U.S.C. § 2339A(b).

48. The federal indictment against John Walker Lindh is available at http://news.findlaw.com/hdocs/docs/terrorism/uswlindh020502cmp.html. The federal indictment against Lynne Stewart is available at http://news.findlaw.com/hdocs/docs/terrorism/ussattar040902ind.pdf.

49. *Humanitarian Law Project v. Reno*, 205 F.3d 1130, 1135–36 (9th Cir. 2000). This suit is currently pending before the Ninth Circuit on appeal from the district court's final order. The author is one of the attorneys representing the Humanitarian Law Project and the remaining plaintiffs in this suit.

50. Ibid.

51. Ibid., 1137–38.

52. 8 U.S.C. § 1189.

53. 8 U.S.C. § 1189(a)(8).

54. See *National Council of Resistance of Iran v. Dept. of State*, 251 F.3d 192 (D.C. Cir. 2001); *People's Mojahedin Org. of Iran v. Dept. of State*, 182 F.3d 17 (D.C. Cir. 1999).

55. *People's Mojahedin Org. of Iran*, 182 F.3d 24.

56. *USA PATRIOT Act* § 411(a), amending 8 U.S.C. §1182(a)(3)(B)(iv)(IV)(bb) and (cc), (V)(bb) and (cc), and (VI)(cc) and (dd). Section 411 of the USA PATRIOT Act is discussed in detail in chapter 2.

57. Tom Brune, "U.S. Evades Curbs in Terror Law," *Newsday*, 26 April 2002, A17.

58. Martin Luther King Jr., "Letter from a Birmingham Jail" (1963), available at http://www.stanford.edu/group/King/frequentdocs/birmingham.pdf.

59. Since 1983, the U.S. government has defined the term "terrorism," "for statistical and analytical purposes," as the "premeditated, politically

motivated violence perpetrated against noncombatant targets by subnational groups or clandestine agents, usually intended to influence an audience." See preface and introduction of *Patterns of Global Terrorism 2001*, U.S. Department of State (May 2002), xvi, available at http://www.state.gov/documents/organization/10286.pdf.

60. *USA PATRIOT Act* § 802, amending 18 U.S.C. § 2331(5).

61. Jim McGee, "Fighting Terror with Databases: Domestic Intelligence Plans Stir Concern," *Washington Post*, 16 February 2002, A27.

62. Ibid.

63. Ibid.

64. *USA PATRIOT Act* § 701, amending 42 U.S.C. § 3796h(c) and (d).

65. *United States Attorney General Guidelines on General Crimes, Racketeering Enterprise and Domestic Security/Terrorism Investigations*, 1989 (Smith guidelines), available at http://usdoj.gov/ag/readingroom/generalcrimea.htm.

66. *United States Attorney General Guidelines on General Crimes, Racketeering Enterprise and Domestic Security/Terrorism Investigations*, 2002 (Ashcroft guidelines), available at http://www.usdoj.gov/olp/generalcrimes2.pdf.

67. *United States Attorney General Guidelines for FBI Foreign Intelligence Collection and Foreign Counterintelligence Investigations* (1995), available at ; Senate Select Committee on Intelligence, the FBI and CISPES, 101st Cong., 1st sess., 1989, 91.

68. Ashcroft guidelines, 10.

69. Ibid., 17.

70. Ibid., 15 (emphasis added).

71. Ibid., 17.

72. Ibid.

73. Ibid., 16.

74. *Brandenberg v. Ohio*, 395 U.S. 444, 447–48, 1969.

75. Ashcroft guidelines, 4–5.

76. Ibid. (emphasis added).

77. Ibid., 17.

78. Ibid., 2.

79. Ibid., 8.

80. Ibid., 18–20.

81. Ibid., 9.

82. Ibid., 9–10

83. Ibid., 7.

84. Ibid.

85. Ibid., 21.

86. Ibid., 21–22.

87. Robert Dreyfuss, "The Cops Are Watching You," *The Nation*, 3 June 2002, 12. See also *Alliance to End Repression v. Rochford*, 407 F.Supp. 115 (N.D. Ill. 1975); *Handschu v. Special Services Division*, 605 F.Supp. 1384 (S.D.N.Y. 1985).

88. Robert Dreyfuss, "The Cops Are Watching You," 14.

89. Ibid.

90. Julie Cart, "Denver Police Spied on Activists, ACLU Says," *Los Angeles Times*, 22 March 2002, A1; "Denver Police Files Raise Rights Concerns," *New York Times*, 14 March 2002.

91. Ibid. A copy of the complaint in *American Friends Service Committee, et al., v. City and County of Denver*, Civil Action No. 02-N-0740 (D. Colo.) (AFSC Complaint), is available at http://www.aclu-co.org/news/complaints/complaint_spyfiles.htm.

92. AFSC Complaint.

93. Ibid.

94. Article III of the U.S. Constitution limits the jurisdiction of the federal courts to actual "cases" and "controversies." In order to have standing to sue in court, a plaintiff must, at a minimum, have suffered, or be threatened with, a specific and direct injury. See *Baker v. Carr*, 369 U.S. 186, 204 (1962) (standing to sue depends on whether the party seeking relief has "alleged such a personal stake in the outcome of the controversy as to assure that concrete adverseness which sharpens the presentation of issues upon which the court so largely depends for illumination of difficult constitutional questions").

95. *Laird v. Tatum*, 408 U.S. 1 (1972).

96. Ibid., 10.

97. Ibid., 13.

98. Ibid.

99. Ibid.

100. *Philadelphia Yearly Meeting v. Tate*, 519 F.2d 1335 (3d Cir. 1975).

101. Ibid., 1338.

102. Ibid.

103. See "Clinton and Reno Memoranda on Administration of Freedom of Information Act," Press Release, Office of the White House Press Secretary, 4 October 1993.

104. Ibid.

105. See Attorney General John Ashcroft, "Memorandum for Heads of All Federal Departments and Agencies" 12 October 2001, available at http://www.usdoj.gov/04foia/011012.htm. See also Ruth Rosen, "The Day Ashcroft Foiled FOIA," *San Francisco Chronicle*, 7 January 2002, D4.

106. Ellen Nakashima, "Bush View of Secrecy Is Stirring Frustration; Disclosure Battle Unites Right and Left," *Washington Post*, 3 March 2002, A4.

107. This issue is discussed in greater detail in chapter 3.

108. See 44 U.S.C. § 2201 et seq.

109. Executive Order 13233, 66 Fed. Reg. 56025 (1 November 2001). See also Steven L. Hansen, "The President's Papers Are the People's Business, *Washington Post*, 16 December 2001.

110. Stanley Kutler, "Classified! George W. Uses 9/11 as Pretext to Reverse the Will of Congress and Wall off Presidential Records," *Chicago Tribune*, 2 January 2002.

111. Ibid.

112. See *American Historical Association v. The National Archives and Records Administration*, No.1:01CV02447 (D. D.C.). Documents in this suit are available at http://www.citizen.org/litigation/briefs/FOIAGovtSec/PresRecords/index.cfm.

113. See William Broad, "U.S. Tightening Rules on Keeping Scientific Secrets," *New York Times*, 17 February 2002, A19.

114. Andrew Card, "Action to Safeguard Information Regarding Weapons of Mass Destruction and Other Sensitive Documents Related to Security Information," available at See also Elizabeth Auster and Tom Diemer, "White House Moves To Hem in Open Records," *Plain Dealer*, 22 March 2002, A8.

115. Ibid.

116. OMB Watch's list of the materials that have been removed from government Web sites since September 11 is available at http://www.omb-watch.org/article/articleview/213/1/104/.

117. Paula Hane, "Removing Information from the Public Web," *Information Today*, 1 May 2002, No. 5, Vol. 19, 56.

118. *New York Times Co. v. United States*, 403 U.S. 713, 717 (1971) (Justices Black and Douglas, concurring).

119. Ibid.

120. Bill Carter and Felicity Barringer, "Networks Agree to U.S. Request to Edit Future bin Laden Tapes," *New York Times*, 11 October2001.

121. Bill Carter, "White House Seeks to Limit Transcripts," *New York Times*, 12 October 2001.

122. Ibid.

123. Matthew Rothschild, "The New McCarthyism."

124. Ibid.

125. James Dao and Eric Schmitt, "Pentagon Readies Efforts to Sway Sentiment Abroad," *New York Times*, 19 February 2002, A1.

126. Ruth Rosen, "Preparing for Perpetual War," *San Francisco Chronicle*, 4 March 2002, B7.

127. Ibid.

128. Art Buchwald, "Truth Dodges a Bullet," *Washington Post*, 5 March 2002, C2.

129. Karen E. Crummy, "Bush Locks Key Lawmakers out of Intelligence Loop," *Boston Herald*, 10 October 2001, 14.

130. See also Jim VandeHei and David Rogers, "Investigation and Mobilization: Bush Directive Limiting Classified Data to Congress after Leak Angers Leaders," *Wall Street Journal*, 10 October 2001, A6.

131. Alison Mitchell, "Letter to Ridge is Latest Jab in Fight Over Balance of Powers," *New York Times*, 5 March 2002, A8.

132. Ibid.

133. Nick Anderson, "Senate Weighs Subpoena to Force Testimony by Ridge," *Boston Globe*, 18 March 2002, A11.

134. Alison Mitchell, "Letter to Ridge."

135. "Daschle Calls for Sharing of Plans: Information Sought in War on Terror." Press Release. 2002 WL 7271824, 4 March 2002.

136. *Whitney v. California*, 274 U.S. 357, 375–376 (1927) (J. Brandeis, concurring).

CHAPTER 5

1. Eve Pell, "Homeland Security x 50," *The Nation*, 3 June 2002.

2. Ibid.

3. See, e.g., *Korematsu v. United States*, 323 U.S. 214 (1944); *Debs. v. United States*, 249 U.S. 211 (1919).

4. Justice William J. Brennan Jr., *The Quest to Develop a Jurisprudence of Civil Liberties in Times of Crisis*, 22 December 1987 (speech delivered at the law school of the Hebrew University in Jerusalem), available at http://www.brennancenter.org/resources/downloads/nation_security_brennan.pdf.

ABOUT THE AUTHOR

NANCY CHANG is the senior litigation attorney at the Center for Constitutional Rights in New York City. Nancy's work at CCR has focused on protecting the First Amendment rights of political activists against government efforts to silence dissent, safeguarding civil liberties against measures taken in the name of national security, protecting the constitutional rights of immigrants, and combating racial profiling.

THE CENTER FOR CONSTITUTIONAL RIGHTS is a nonprofit legal and educational organization dedicated to protecting and advancing the rights guaranteed by the United States Constitution and the Universal Declaration of Human Rights. CCR's work began in 1966 with the legal representation of civil rights activists in the Jim Crow South. Over the last four decades, CCR has played an important role in many popular movements for peace and social justice. CCR uses litigation proactively to combat government efforts to suppress political dissent, to advance the law in a positive direction, to empower poor communities and communities of color, to train the next generation of constitutional and human rights attorneys, and to strengthen the broader movement for constitutional and human rights.

As our nation formulates a response to the terrorist attacks on September 11, CCR believes that clamping down on civil liberties at home and relying on the instruments of war and violence abroad are not the answers. Hence, in this moment of national crisis, CCR will remain true to its vision, values, and principles, vigorously promoting civil rights and human rights, social justice and social change, and the expansion of political and economic democracy as the best prescription for creating a just, humane, peaceful, and secure nation and world. Toward this end, we regard freedom of speech and the right to assemble peacefully without fear of harassment and intimidation by the government as an indispensable cornerstone of our democracy and a vital channel for the articulation of dissent. CCR will exercise its First Amendment rights toward the goals of defending our civil liberties and advancing the peaceful resolution of conflicts at this critical hour in our nation's history.

Center for Constitutional Rights
666 Broadway, 7th Floor
New York, New York 10012
(212) 614-6464 | www.ccr-ny.org

Nancy Chang